HISPANIC AMERICAN BIOGRAPHY

Volume I: A-K

Rob Nagel and Sharon Rose, *Editors*

An imprint of Gale Research Inc.,
an International Thomson Publishing Company

I(T)P

NEW YORK • LONDON • BONN • BOSTON • DETROIT • MADRID
MELBOURNE • MEXICO CITY • PARIS • SINGAPORE • TOKYO
TORONTO • WASHINGTON • ALBANY NY • BELMONT CA • CINCINNATI OH

HISPANIC AMERICAN BIOGRAPHY

Rob Nagel and Sharon Rose, *Editors*

Staff

Sonia Benson, *U·X·L Associate Developmental Editor*
Carol DeKane Nagel, *U·X·L Developmental Editor*
Thomas L. Romig, *U·X·L Publisher*

Arlene Johnson, *Permissions Associate (Pictures)*
Margaret A. Chamberlain, *Permissions Supervisor (Pictures)*

Mary Kelley, *Production Associate*
Evi Seoud, *Assistant Production Manager*
Mary Beth Trimper, *Production Director*

Mary Krzewinski, *Cover and Page Designer*
Cynthia Baldwin, *Art Director*

This book is printed on acid-free paper that meets the minimum requirements of American National Standard for Information Sciences—Permanence Paper for Printed Library Materials, ANSI Z39.48-1984.

ISBN 0-8103-9828-1 (Set)
ISBN 0-8103-9824-9 (Volume 1)
ISBN 0-8103-9825-7 (Volume 2)

Printed in the United States of America

I(T)P™ U·X·L is an imprint of Gale Research Inc.,
an International Thomson Publishing Company.
ITP logo is a trademark under license.

CONTENTS

READER'S GUIDE

Hispanic American Biography profiles more than 90 Hispanic Americans, both living and deceased, prominent in fields ranging from civil rights to athletics, politics to literature, entertainment to science, religion to the military. The volumes also include Spanish founders and early leaders of Hispanic America as well as central figures of contemporary Hispanic cultural movements in the United States and in Latin America. A black-and-white portrait accompanies each entry, and a list of sources for further reading or research is provided at the end of each entry. Cross-references to other profiles in these volumes are noted in bold letters within the text. The volumes are arranged alphabetically and conclude with an index listing all individuals by fields of endeavor.

Related reference sources:

Hispanic American Almanac explores the history and culture of Hispanic America, a community of people in the United States whose ancestors—or they themselves—came from Spain or from the Spanish-speaking countries of South and Central America, Mexico, Puerto Rico, or Cuba. The *Almanac* is organized into 14 subject chapters, including immigration, family and religion, jobs and education, literature, and sports. The volume contains more than 70 black-and-white photographs and maps, a glossary, and a cumulative subject index.

Hispanic American Chronology explores significant social, political, economic, cultural, and educational milestones in Hispanic American history. Arranged by year and then by month and day, the chronology spans from 1492 to modern times and contains more than 70 illustrations, extensive cross references, and a cumulative subject index.

Hispanic American Voices presents full or excerpted speeches, sermons, orations, poems, testimony, and other notable spoken works of Hispanic Americans. Each entry is accompanied by an introduction and boxes explaining terms and events to which the speech refers. The volume contains pertinent black-and-white illustrations and a cumulative subject index.

Advisors

Special thanks are due for the invaluable comments and suggestions provided by U•X•L's Hispanic American books advisors:

Margarita Reichounia
Librarian, Bowen Branch
Detroit Public Library

Linda Garcia
Librarian, Southern Hills Middle School
Boulder, Colorado

Comments and Suggestions

We welcome your comments on *Hispanic American Biography* as well as your suggestions for topics to be featured in future editions. Please write: Editors, *Hispanic American Biography,* U•X•L, 835 Penobscot Bldg., Detroit, Michigan 48226-4094; call toll-free: 1-800-877-4253; or fax: 313-961-6348.

PICTURE CREDITS

Linda Alvarado

Business owner
Born in 1951, Albuquerque, New Mexico

"Baseball has been a sport in which Hispanics have achieved tremendous success. And in that regard, many role models and outstanding individuals have emerged as players."

Linda Alvarado

L inda Alvarado has never let tradition influence her career path. As the only girl in a family of six children, she grew up competing with boys. Years later, she is still doing so as a female executive of a business usually run by males. She is president of her own building company, Alvarado Construction, Inc., and a limited partner in the ownership group of the Colorado Rockies, a major league baseball team that played its first season in 1993. "As the first Hispanic woman to enter the dugout," Milton Jamail pointed out in *Hispanic,* "some Hispanics see her as someone who can make a difference for the fans and players of this all-American sport."

Born Linda B. Martinez in 1951, she grew up in Albuquerque, New Mexico. Her father worked for the Atomic Energy Commission, and her mother was a homemaker. "It was a very positive environment," she told Carol Hopkins in *Notable Hispanic American Women.* "Even though I was the only girl, the expectation for me was no different." She credits her parents with giving her confidence and self-esteem and encouraging her to excel in the classroom and in

athletics. Active in both high school and college sports, she played basketball, volleyball, and softball, and also ran track.

Launches Construction Career

After Alvarado graduated from California's Pomona College, she continued to work as a lab assistant in the college's botany department. Her stay there was brief, however, as she "overwatered and drowned all the plants," she told Hopkins. She then took a job with a California development company and learned all about the construction business, from preparing bids for a building project to writing a contract for the actual work. Much to her surprise, Alvarado found she liked the work. She returned to school and took classes in estimating, blueprint reading, and scheduling to expand her knowledge of the construction business.

In 1974 Alvarado and a partner started the Martinez Alvarado Construction Management Corporation in Denver, Colorado. Within two years, she bought out her partner and soon became a general contractor (the person or company in charge of hiring and organizing all the carpenters, electricians, plumbers, and other tradespeople on a building project). Since that time, her company—now known as Alvarado Construction, Inc.—has completed dozens of large-scale building projects, including office buildings, bus stations, airport hangars, and a convention center. These accomplishments fill Alvarado with a sense of pride. "There is enormous satisfaction," she told Hopkins, "knowing that one started from ground zero and has a terrific final project, something of great permanence and beauty."

Invests in Major League Baseball

In the early 1990s, Alvarado was able to turn her life-long interest in sports into a business opportunity. She became a partner in the Colorado Rockies baseball team because she wanted to show that women can get involved in nontraditional fields. She also believed it was important to give something back to the city of Denver. "I really felt it was in the best interest of my company to support the community in a more substantial way," she explained to Jamail.

Perhaps the main reason Alvarado chose to invest in baseball is its record of providing Hispanics with a road to accomplishment. "Baseball has been a sport in which Hispanics have achieved tremendous success," she pointed out to Jamail. "And in that regard, many role models and outstanding individuals have emerged as players." As a Hispanic owner, Alvarado believes she has now brought that sense of accomplishment full circle.

Alvarado is a member of the board of directors of several other large companies. Boards of directors are groups of businesspeople who help a company make decisions and choose leaders. Recognizing the inroads she has made as a Hispanic and as a woman, Alvarado is mindful of those who helped pave the way before her and those who will follow afterward. Whenever she has had to resign from a board, Alvarado recommends another Hispanic or woman to replace her. "I'm not there because I'm good," she told Hopkins. "I'm there because someone ahead of me was great."

For Further Information

Hispanic, April 1993, pp. 18-22.
Notable Hispanic American Women, Gale Research, 1993, pp. 11-12.

Rudolfo Anaya

Writer, college professor
Born October 30, 1937, Pastura, New Mexico

"Each community has art to offer, and now we've come to a place in American history where we celebrate that."

Rudolfo Alfonso Anaya is hailed as one of the founding fathers of Chicano (Mexican American) literature. He has been a prolific writer for over two decades, publishing novels, short stories, plays, poetry, and screenplays. Anaya draws on the memories of his childhood in New Mexico, as well as on Mexican folklore, to portray the experiences of Hispanics in the American Southwest. Many critics believe his first novel, *Bless Me, Ultima,* most successfully presents those experiences. Quickly becoming a prize-winning best-seller after it was published in 1972, the novel is now required reading for many high school and college students.

Anaya was born in 1937 in the small rural village of Pastura, New Mexico. His mother, Rafaelita Mares, had come from a family of farmers. His father, Martin Anaya, was a *vaquero,* an expert horseman who enjoyed working with cattle. Carrying on their strong Mexican heritage, the family spoke only Spanish at home. "As far as I knew," Anaya wrote in his short autobiography in *Contemporary Authors Autobiography Series,* "all of the world spoke Spanish."

When Anaya was still a young boy, his family moved to the nearby town of Santa Rosa. Going to public school, where only English was spoken, was at first a frightening experience for him, but he quickly became a good student. Throughout grade school, he enjoyed the company of a group of close friends. By the eighth grade, however, he began to notice changes in the group. "Prejudices I had not known before appeared," he wrote in his autobiography. "We who had always been brothers now separated into Anglos [whites] and Mexicans. I did not understand the process."

Diving Accident Causes Temporary Paralysis

When Anaya was 15, his family moved to a barrio (a Spanish-speaking neighborhood) in Albuquerque, New Mexico. Shortly thereafter, he experienced an event that changed his life: in a frightening diving accident, he fractured two neck vertebrae and was paralyzed. He described the experience in his autobiography: "I floated to the top of the water, opened my eyes, saw the light of the sun shining in the water. I tried to move, I couldn't. Face down, my shouts for help were only bubbles of water." Anaya was pulled from the water by a friend and spent months in therapy to regain the use of his legs. He recovered from the accident with a greater appreciation for life, determined to do more than his healthy friends had ever done.

In 1956 Anaya graduated from Albuquerque High School. He attended Browning Business School for two years, but dropped out because he found the study of business unfulfilling. He then enrolled in the University of New Mexico to study English. While there, he began to question why he never had any Mexican teachers and why he never read any Mexican literature. He felt the education he received did not reflect the long history of Hispanics in the southwestern United States.

Another question that plagued Anaya at this time was one of faith. He had been raised a devout Catholic, but his readings at the university caused him to question his religious beliefs. In turn, this loss of faith led him to write poetry and prose. "I lost my faith in God," he wrote in his autobiography, "and if there was no God there was no meaning, no secure road to salvation.... That may

Rudolfo Anaya

be why I write. It is easier to ascribe those times and their bittersweet emotions to my characters."

Love of Art Fostered in Childhood

Anaya believes he was further drawn to writing because his warm, tradition-filled childhood filled him with a love for art. He cited examples of art that surrounded him in the homes of his youth: detailed carvings in door frames, brightly painted walls, decorative altars, lively music, and melodic language. "There is something in the Mexican character which, even under the most oppressive circumstances, struggles to keep art and its humanizing effect alive…. The Mexican possesses a very artistic soul," he wrote in *Contemporary Authors Autobiography Series.*

After he graduated from college in 1963, Anaya became a public school teacher in Albuquerque. Three years later he married Patricia Lawless. In 1971, after having earned master's degrees in English and in guidance and counseling, Anaya became the director of counseling at the University of New Mexico in Albuquerque. A few years later he began teaching creative writing and Chicano literature in the university's English department. He maintained a position in this department for the next 19 years, until his retirement in 1993.

During the 1960s, Anaya began work on his novel *Bless Me, Ultima.* Haunted by the Mexican American stories and tales of his childhood, he tried to capture the memory of those times and people. He worked on the story for seven years, then endured rejection by dozens of publishers. In 1972 Anaya finally found a Chicano publishing house in California that wanted to publish the book. *Bless Me, Ultima* was an instant success. The novel was honored with the prestigious Premio Quinto Sol Award, given annually to the best novel written by a Chicano author. Anaya became a celebrity.

Novel Explores Young Boy's Struggles

Bless Me, Ultima follows the life of Antonio, a young boy growing up in a small village in New Mexico around the time of World War II. As he matures, Antonio struggles to understand the roles of good and evil in life. He also has to choose between the nomadic (wandering) lifestyle of his father's family and the farming lifestyle of his mother's family. Throughout the novel, a folk healer named Ultima tries to bring harmony and well-being to Antonio and his family.

Anaya continued to use Mexican American myth and folklore in his next two novels, *Heart of Aztlán* (1976) and *Tortuga* (1979). *Heart of Aztlán* describes a Mexican American family's move from a rural area to a barrio in Albuquerque—and the problems, both social and religious, they face adjusting to city life. (Aztlán is the mythological land of origin of the Aztec people. Many Mexican Americans believe it occupied the geographic region now known as the American Southwest.) *Tortuga* tells the story of a 16-year-old boy who is paralyzed. Because he has to wear a shell-like body cast, his friends call him Tortuga (Spanish for "turtle"). While recovering in a hospital for a year, Tortuga becomes more spiritually and psychologically mature.

Anaya's first three novels drew upon his real-life experiences, and his later works continued to center on issues of faith and the loss of faith. With his focus on Mexican American myths and cultural awareness, Anaya has remained a profound presence in the field of Chicano literature since the 1970s.

In 1994 Anaya finally received major recognition when he signed a contract with Warner Books to publish six books. As part of the deal, Warner agreed to publish both mass market paperback and color-illustrated hardcover editions of *Bless Me, Ultima*. Warner also decided to publish a Spanish edition of the novel, making it the first time this major company had ever released a Spanish-language book. Anaya was ulti-

mately pleased to have the chance to present his culture to a mainstream audience. "Each community has art to offer," he explained in *Publishers Weekly*, "and now we've come to a place in American history where we can celebrate that."

For Further Information

Contemporary Authors Autobiography Series, Volume 4, Gale, 1986, pp. 15-28.
English Journal, September 1992, pp. 20+.
Hispanic Writers, Gale, 1991, pp. 24-26.
Publishers Weekly, March 21, 1994, p. 24.

Desi Arnaz

Bandleader, actor, producer
Born March 2, 1917, Santiago, Cuba
Died December 2, 1986, Del Mar, California

"[Arnaz was] a man who lived the immigrant dream. It's such a great dream, and an absolutely true story." —Laurence Luckinbill, Back Stage

Desi Arnaz achieved fame and fortune playing the hassled husband to his real-life wife on the long-running television series *I Love Lucy*. His character, Ricky Ricardo, was loosely based on his real role as a Cuban bandleader married to a zany American beauty. Behind the scenes, he was a talented producer, director, musician, and businessman.

He was born Desiderio Alberto Arnaz y De Acha III on March 2, 1917, in Santiago, Cuba. His father was mayor of the city and was quite wealthy. The elder Arnaz had plans for his son to study law at the University of Notre Dame in South Bend, Indiana, then return to Cuba to practice. Those plans drastically changed on August 12, 1933. Fulgencio Batista y Zaldívar, a sergeant in the Cuban army, led a revolt that overthrew the president of Cuba, Gerardo Machado. During the takeover, Arnaz's father was jailed, and all of his money and property were seized.

Arnaz, 16 years old at the time, fled with his mother to Miami, Florida. His father joined them after he was released six months later. Arnaz spoke hardly any English and had to struggle through classes at St. Patrick's High School in Miami. At night, he helped support his family through a variety of jobs: cleaning birdcages, working in a railyard, bookkeeping, and driving taxis.

Since his dream of attending law school was lost, Arnaz tried for a career in music. In 1937 he auditioned and was hired as a singer at the Roney Plaza Hotel in Miami Beach. While touring through Miami with his orchestra, famed bandleader Xavier Cugat saw Arnaz perform. Impressed, Cugat asked the young singer to join his group.

Feels Greatest Pleasure Playing Music

After a year with Cugat, Arnaz left to form his own Latin dance band. The group quickly became successful and played at some of the best nightclubs in the United States, including New York City's famed Copacabana. Laurence Luckinbill, who would become Arnaz's son-in-law, told Amy Hersh of *Back Stage* years later that Arnaz "was a man who was not alive unless he was playing music. It was a way out for him, the way he conquered fear and gave the most pleasure to those who knew him."

The director George Abbot saw Arnaz perform at the Copacabana one evening in 1939 and offered the singer the leading role in his Broadway musical *Too Many Girls*. The following year, a studio in Hollywood made a film version of the play with Arnaz recreating his role. The female lead was played by an actress named Lucille Ball.

Despite having careers that often put them at opposite ends of the United States, Arnaz and Ball fell in love. On November 30, 1940, after Arnaz's band finished its last set in a New York nightclub, Arnaz and Ball drove to Greenwich, Connecticut, and were married by a justice of the peace. Over the next ten years, the couple was hardly together. Arnaz made a few movies, including *Father Takes a Wife* and *Holiday in Havana,* but mostly he toured the country with his orchestra. Meanwhile, Ball worked on her successful radio program, *My Favorite Husband.*

The Beginning of Television History

In 1950 the couple had the idea of turning *My Favorite Husband* into a television show. Ball wanted Arnaz to play her husband in the series, but CBS network producers did not accept the idea. They thought Americans would not watch a show about an all-American woman married to a Cuban man who led an orchestra. To prove CBS wrong, Arnaz and Ball went on tour across the country as a husband-and-wife comedy team. Each successive performance drew a larger and larger audience. Finally convinced, CBS let Arnaz and Ball have their television show. *I Love Lucy* went on the air in the fall of 1951.

The show was an instant success. During its first six years, *I Love Lucy* always ranked in the top three television shows. In the series, Arnaz played the straight-man to his wife's hilarious character, and often performed a Latin musical number as part of the show. In addition to acting in front of the camera, Arnaz worked behind it as head of Desilu Productions, the couple's production team. Among the other popular television shows he helped produce were *The Danny Thomas Show, Our Miss Brooks,* and *The Untouchables.* Arnaz is credited with the idea of using three cameras to record each episode, which allowed for fine editing afterward. This technique is still used to film situation comedies on television.

Fortune Follows

Desilu Productions became an entertainment empire. It owned a record company, a music-publishing firm, motion picture and television studios, real estate in California, and the Desi Arnaz Western Hills Hotel in Palm Springs. In 1958 Arnaz and Ball sold 190 episodes of *I Love Lucy* to CBS for six million dollars. Because Arnaz insisted on filming the show rather than performing it live, high-quality copies of each episode existed for endless reruns. The show is still televised daily around the world.

Arnaz and Ball had two children, Lucie and Desi, Jr., both of whom work in the entertainment business. Arnaz and Ball's marriage, however, was not happy. In 1960 the couple divorced. Two years later Arnaz sold his share of Desilu to Ball for three million dollars and went into semiretirement on his horse farm in Del Mar, California. The following year he married Edith Mack Hirsch.

Desi Arnaz

Over the next 20 years, Arnaz occasionally worked on television productions. He helped create several series pilots and the comedy series *The Mothers-in-Law* (1967-69). In 1982 he played a dramatic role in *The Escape Artist,* a film directed by Francis Ford Coppola. Poor health marked his later years, and he died from lung cancer at his home in 1986. Luckinbill told Hersh he would always remember Arnaz as "a man who lived the immigrant dream. It's such a great dream, and an absolutely true story."

For Further Information

Andrews, Bart, *The "I Love Lucy" Book,* Doubleday, 1985.

Arnaz, Desi, *A Book,* William Morrow, 1976.

Back Stage, February 8, 1991, pp. 33, 43.

New York Times, December 3, 1986, p. D26.

People, February 18, 1991, pp. 84-95.

Judith Baca

Artist, muralist, professor
Born September 20, 1946, Los Angeles,
  California

*"If we cannot imagine peace as an active
concept, how can we ever hope for it to
happen?"*

Judith Francisca Baca started her career as an artist by creating colorful murals (large wall paintings) to decorate the city of Los Angeles. Her work reflects her deep interest in social problems (particularly those dealing with race) and has earned her international attention. Her best-known work is *The Great Wall of Los Angeles,* a half-mile-long outdoor mural—the largest in the world. In addition to her work as a muralist, Baca helped found the Social and Public Art Resource Center (SPARC) in Venice, California, an organization that fosters the development of Hispanic artists.

Baca was born September 20, 1946, in south-central Los Angeles. A second-generation Chicana (Mexican American woman), she was raised in a strong female household with her mother, grandmother, and two aunts, one of whom was mentally retarded. She did not know her musician father well, but enjoyed a happy childhood. "It was a very strong, wonderful, matriarchal [mother as leader] household," she related to Yleana Martinez in *Notable Hispanic American Women.* "I was everybody's child. I had a wonderful playmate in my grown-up aunt

who wasn't grown up in her head. It was like she was five, my age, only she was big."

When Baca was six, she moved with her mother to Pacoima, California. Since she had spent most of her childhood in a Spanish-speaking household, she had a difficult time adjusting to school, where only English was spoken. She often felt alone in the classroom. However, during this time her interest in art developed when one of her teachers allowed her to sit in a corner and paint while the rest of the class carried on.

After graduating from a Catholic high school in 1964, Baca enrolled in California State University in Northridge. She earned a bachelor's degree in art in 1969, then returned to her high school to teach. She tried out her first cooperative art project that year when she rounded up a group of ethnically diverse students to paint a mural at the school. It was "a method to force the group into cooperation," she told Martinez. It would come to be a method she would use many times in future projects.

Fired for War Protests

At this same time Baca became active in the peace movement against the war in Vietnam. She and many nuns who taught at the high school participated in marches. Her school's administration, however, did not approve of these antiwar activities and fired all of those teachers involved. Left with no job, Baca feared her teaching career was over.

Baca soon found a position in a special program for artists with the City of Los Angeles Cultural Affairs Division. Her new job required her to travel to schools and parks to teach art. In those areas, she noticed the art

Judith Baca standing in front of "Triumph of the Hearts," a panel from *World Wall*

the teenagers had already created. "As she observed the graffiti, the tattoos, and the decorated cars," Anne Estrada noted in *Hispanic,* "she recognized a visual language used by these teenagers to express who they were and how they feel about their lives." Hoping to bring these teenagers together, she formed her own painting group, "Las Vistas Nuevas." The group—made up of 20 kids from different gangs and neighborhood groups—soon worked together to paint Baca's first mural, in Hollenbeck Park.

Inspired by Mexican Muralists

Around this time, Baca began to study the Mexican tradition of mural painting and some of its great artists, including Diego Rivera (see **Diego Rivera**) and José Clemente Orozco. She traveled to Mexico to take classes in mural materials and techniques and to look at the mural works of Mexico's masters. She told Martinez that, like those Mexican artists who came before her, "I believe taking art to the people is a political act. I am a Mexican mural painter in the true sense, but I took it to the next level. To keep an art form living it has to grow and change."

Baca returned to Los Angeles and expanded her program into the Citywide Mural Project. Under her supervision, almost 250 murals were painted. Baca was the first in the city to work with a multicultural group of youth to produce murals. Her most ambitious project during the 1970s was the *Great Wall,* painted on the walls of a San Fernando Valley drainage canal. The half-mile-long mural depicts the city's multiethnic history with a series of pictures showing important events from the Stone Age to the 1950s. Baca developed the concept, hired the workers, and helped raise the money for the project. Some of the teenagers who worked on the project did so to fulfill court sentences. The Great Wall took five summers, spread out over a period of nine years, to complete.

In 1976 Baca founded the Social and Public Art Resource Center (SPARC) in Venice, California. The nonprofit, multicultural art center brings together artists, community groups, and youth groups to create murals and preserve other public art. SPARC is an internationally recognized center that also keeps a library of 16,000 slides of public art from around the world.

Begins Work on World Wall

In 1987 Baca began an even grander project—*World Wall: A Vision of the Future Without Fear.* The work addresses issues of war, peace, cooperation, interdependence, and spiritual growth. Its images depict the changes—both spiritual and material—that must occur on the planet before world harmony can be achieved. The portable mural is made of seven 10-by-30-foot panels painted by Baca. In 1990, when four of the panels were finished, the mural was displayed in Finland. It then traveled to the Soviet Union for viewing. The finished mural will include another seven panels to be painted by artists from the countries in which it is displayed.

Baca, who is a full professor of art at the University of California at Irvine, believes her art reflects her commitment to help solve social problems. Whether on a local or a global level, she tries to inspire people to act on the positive possibilities in life. In her artist's statement for *World Wall,* she wrote that people have an easier time imagining a world caught in nuclear war than one that exists in perfect peace. She believes we must be able to imagine and picture peace in order to achieve it. "If we cannot imagine peace as an active concept," she wrote, "how can we ever hope for it to happen?"

For Further Information

Hispanic, May 1991, pp. 16-18.

Lippard, Lucy, *Mixed Blessings: Art for a Multicultural America,* Penguin Books, 1988.

Notable Hispanic American Women, Gale Research, 1993, pp. 35-38.

Joan Baez

Singer, songwriter, activist
Born January 9, 1941, Staten Island, New York

"I have been true to the principles of nonviolence, developing a stronger and stronger aversion to the ideologies of both the far right and the far left and ... [to] the suffering they continue to produce all over the world."

Often called the "Queen of the Folksingers," Joan Baez has earned fame as much for her political activism as for her singing. During the 1960s, she often made headlines by using her musical talent to campaign against America's involvement in the Vietnam War and against social injustice. Through her music, writings, and travels, she has continued her fight against social ills—not only in America but around the world—to the present day.

Joan Chandos Baez was born in 1941 on Staten Island, New York. From her Scottish mother, Joan Bridge, and her Mexican father, Albert Baez, she inherited a rich multiethnic tradition. She also inherited their nonviolent Quaker religious beliefs, which would eventually inspire her own interests in peace and justice. Baez's father was a physicist who once turned down a high-paying job developing war weapons because of his moral concerns. In her 1987 autobiography, *And a Voice to Sing With,* Baez wrote that her father's decision left an imprint on his children. She and her sisters "would never have all the fine things little girls want when they are growing up. Instead we would have a father with a clear conscience. Decency would be his legacy to us."

Exposed to Racism Early in Life

While growing up, Baez was often taunted by other children because of her Hispanic roots and dark skin. In junior high school she felt isolated from her classmates. "So there I was," she wrote in her autobiography, "with a Mexican name, skin, and hair: the Anglos couldn't accept me because of all three, and the Mexicans couldn't accept me because I didn't speak Spanish." Her pacifist (antiwar) views further distanced her from her classmates.

In large part, loneliness led Baez to begin singing. Believing music to be a path to popularity, she spent a summer developing her voice and learning to play the ukulele. She soon gained a reputation as an entertainer and made her first stage appearance in a school talent show. She also became known to her peers as a talented artist who could draw Disney characters and paint school election posters with ease.

In 1958 Baez graduated from high school, then moved with her family to Boston, Massachusetts, after her father had accepted a teaching position at the Massachusetts Institute of Technology. Although she enrolled in Boston University, Baez's interest in her music kept her away from her classes. Due to such singers and groups as Pete Seeger and the Kingston Trio, folk music was undergoing a revival during the late 1950s. Coffee houses that featured local singers became gathering spots for college students throughout the country. When Baez began singing in

Joan Baez

known for its quality classical music recordings. Her first solo album, simply titled *Joan Baez,* was released in 1960. Composed of traditional folk songs, the album notably featured both a Scottish ballad and a song sung in Spanish—a nod to the ethnic roots of her parents.

Around the time the album was released, Baez moved to California's Pacific coast. During the next three years, she toured the country performing concerts. As she grew increasingly popular, Baez began to think more about the world and her place in it. "I was in a position now to do something more with my life than just sing," she wrote in *And a Voice to Sing With.* "I had the capacity to make lots and lots of money. I could reach lots and lots of people."

Baez used her celebrity status to publicize her views on equal rights and pacifism. When she discovered that African Americans were not admitted to her concerts at white colleges in the South, she organized her own tour of performances at black colleges. To protest the Vietnam War, Baez refused to pay the portion of her federal income taxes she believed went to support the war effort. A rising national leader in the growing protest movements of the 1960s, Baez soon considered her work for social change more important than her performing career.

Boston-area coffee houses, she quickly attracted a large following of fans.

Makes Professional Debut Before Thousands

While singing at a Chicago nightclub in 1959, Baez caught the attention of Bob Gibson, a popular folksinger. Impressed, he asked her to appear with him at the first Newport (California) Folk/Jazz Festival being held in August of that year. Baez's three-octave soprano voice and down-to-earth stage presence captivated the festival crowd of 13,000. She became a celebrity overnight. Many large record companies offered her recording contracts, but she chose to sign her first contract with Vanguard, a small label

Jailed for Political Demonstrations

While Baez's pacifist activities drew praise and wholehearted support from some, they also drew anger from others. U.S. Army bases all over the world banned her albums. In 1967 she was jailed for her part in antiwar demonstrations. The following year she married David Harris, another leader in the war resistance movement. Despite the criticism she received for her political activities, she maintained her enormous popularity as a singer because of the power of her voice and the sincerity of the message in her songs.

In one of the highlights of her career, Baez performed at the famous Woodstock Music Festival, held near Bethel, New York, during the summer of 1969. The five-day event brought together some of the most important popular musicians of the decade. The concert, with its theme of "five days of peace, love, and music," drew more than 500,000 people from all over America.

Through the 1970s, despite having a son (she divorced her husband in 1971), Baez managed to continue her musical career and her social and political activities. "The Night They Drove Old Dixie Down," a cut off her album *Blessed Are...*, became one of the most popular songs of 1972 and Baez's biggest commercial hit. That same year she organized a gathering of women and children who joined hands around the Congress building in Washington, D.C., to protest the continued U.S. involvement in the war in Vietnam. Baez also joined and began working for Amnesty International, a worldwide organization that helps to free people who have been imprisoned for their religious or political beliefs. In 1979 Baez founded Humanitas International, an organization that promotes human rights and nonviolence through education.

Social Cause Revives Career

Baez's popularity began to decline in the early 1980s. However, her career received a boost in 1985 when she opened the U.S. portion of Live Aid, the multi-act rock concert that raised money for famine victims in Ethiopia. In 1987 Baez released *Recently,* her first album in eight years, and published *And a Voice to Sing With.* In her autobiography she wrote about her disappointment in a new generation of young people who seemed more interested in obtaining materials things than in helping others.

Hoping to set an example for younger generations, Baez has continued her activism, something of which she is proud. "I have been true to the principles of nonviolence," she wrote in her autobiography, "developing a stronger and stronger aversion to the ideologies of both the far right and the far left and ... [to] the suffering they continue to produce all over the world." In 1988 she toured the Middle East, hoping to find solutions to the conflicts between the area's warring countries. In 1991 she announced plans to develop low-income housing in California. Two years later she toured the city of Sarajevo in war-torn Bosnia and Hercegovina (part of the former Yugoslavia).

Baez's powerful and wide-ranging voice is what first brought her fame, and it has endured well throughout the years. In an early review in the *New York Times,* Bob Shelton wrote that her voice was "as lustrous and rich as old gold." In an article for the *New York Times* 28 years later, Stephen Holden wrote that Baez's voice, "though quite different in texture from the ethereal folk soprano of her first albums, remains a powerful instrument." Baez's 1993 release, *Play Me Backwards,* was nominated for a Grammy award for best contemporary folk album. Many critics considered it the best album of her long career.

For Further Information

Baez, Joan, *Daybreak,* Dial Press, 1968.

Baez, Joan, *And a Voice to Sing With,* Summit Books, 1987.

Garza, Hedda, *Joan Baez,* Chelsea House, 1991.

New York Times, November 13, 1961; December 12, 1989, p. C24.

Lourdes G. Baird

U.S. attorney
Born May 12, 1935, Quito, Ecuador

"As a U.S. attorney in California, Baird presides over the largest federal judicial district in the nation."

A fter having married and raised three children, Lourdes G. Baird decided to change her life. She went back to school to prepare for a new career as a lawyer. She soon rose through the legal ranks to became one of the handful of women in the United States who serve as federal prosecutors (lawyers representing the U.S. government in cases involving federal crimes). As a U.S. attorney in California, Baird presides over the largest federal judicial district in the nation. Even though she began her work as a lawyer and a judge late in life, she made her mark quickly and has been widely praised for her abilities.

Baird was born in Ecuador in 1935, the seventh child of James Gillespie and Josefina Delgado. Her family moved from South America to Los Angeles when she was just one year old. Because her mother was a devout Catholic, Baird was educated in Catholic, all-girl schools. She has said that her all-girl high school was a great experience. The nuns in charge were positive role models who passed on their independent spirit to the students in the classroom and on the athletic field. To this day, Baird remains physically active in such sports as hiking, jogging, and cross-country skiing.

After graduating from high school, Baird briefly attended secretarial school. In 1956 she married businessman William Baird. Together they had three children: William, Jr., Maria, and John. Baird stayed home to take care of the children for 11 years. When her youngest child entered school, she decided it was time to resume her education as well.

Goes Back to School

Much older than her fellow students, Baird was nervous about attending Los Angeles City College. As she went along, however, she gained confidence. After attending the college for five years as a part-time student, Baird earned her associate of arts degree in 1971. She then transferred to the University of California at Los Angeles and began work on a bachelor's degree in sociology. By 1973 she had earned her degree and had been accepted to law school at the same university. Her marriage came to an end in 1975, but Baird continued with her legal studies. After she graduated in 1976, she took the bar exam (an examination that allows lawyers to practice) and passed it on her first attempt.

Over the next 12 years, Baird moved up steadily through various city, county, and state court levels. She was hired right out of law school to work as an assistant prosecutor in the United States Attorney's Office in California. In 1983 she worked as a private lawyer in a prestigious Los Angeles law firm. Three years later California governor George Deukmejian appointed Baird to a Los Angeles Municipal Court judgeship. In 1988 the governor promoted Baird to the position of Los Angeles County Superior Court judge.

During this period Baird was heavily involved in social and civic organizations. She worked for the California Women Lawyers Association, was president of her college alumni group, served on legal advisory committees, and was active in several Hispanic legal organizations.

Nominated for U.S. Attorney Position

In 1989 California senator Pete Wilson nominated Baird to fill the position of U.S. attorney for the Central District of California. Some 12 million people live in the district, making the position one of the most powerful in the country. What was unusual about her nomination was that she was a Democrat and Wilson was a Republican. But Baird's legal work had made her well known throughout the state, and members of both political parties praised her nomination.

In order for Baird to be placed in the position, she had to win the consent of President George Bush, the U.S. Senate, and the Federal Bureau of Investigation. Her qualifications, career, judicial decisions, and reputation were carefully investigated and evaluated. Eight months passed before she was cleared and approved for the position in 1990.

Lourdes G. Baird

Focuses on Drugs

As U.S. attorney for the Central District of California, Baird is responsible for a staff of more than 140 lawyers. Her department handles the federal legal problems of the largest district in the nation, one that is filled with crime. Baird's immediate focus was on drug abuse. During her time as a judge, she observed that illegal drugs were the reason behind the majority of crimes brought before her. "Crime is rampant," she told Henry Weinstein of the *Los Angeles Times.* "My experience on the bench has indicated to me the horror of drugs—the main problem in the United States." Baird's stand on crime is a tough one—she firmly believes in the death penalty in certain situations. But she also believes more treatment facilities are needed in the country to help aid those who have drug problems.

In April 1992 Baird's office was thrust into one of the biggest legal cases in the United States in the 1990s—the Rodney King trial. A year before, a black motorist named Rodney King had been chased and stopped by several white Los Angeles police officers. An 81-second videotape showed that the police officers had beaten King savagely after he was stopped. Four officers were brought to trial for the beating, but a jury found them not guilty. The verdict in the case set off a riot in Los Angeles, one of the worst ever recorded in the United States. Sixty people died and property damage totaled more than $800 million.

After the riot, Baird headed up a new prosecution of the officers, this time for having violated King's civil rights—a federal offense. Although Baird did not personally handle the prosecution in court, her administrative skills figured prominently in the case. In April 1993 two of the officers—Laurence Powell and Stacy Koon—were found guilty and sentenced to jail.

For Further Information

Detroit Free Press, August 6, 1992, p. 3A.
Los Angeles Times, November 30, 1989, p. B1; December 4, 1989, p. B6; July 19, 1990, p. B1.
Wall Street Journal, April 19, 1993, p. A1.

Rubén Blades

Singer, actor, lawyer, politician
Born July 16, 1948, Panama City, Panama

"A country is not abandoned because we are far from its territory, a country is abandoned when we remove it from our heart."

Rubén Blades is a multi-talented celebrity whose interests range from music to film to politics. He grew up in Panama City, Panama, but immigrated to New York in 1974 with only $100 in his pocket. During the next 20 years, he became an international entertainer and earned a law degree from Harvard University. Although Blades has often been separated from his native Panama, his interests have remained with its government and its people. In May 1994 he made a strong run for the presidency of his homeland.

Blades's parents met in the 1940s while both were performers in Panama City nightclubs. His mother, Anoland Benita, was a cabaret singer while his father, Rubén Dario Blades, was a conga player in a band. Born in 1948 in a poor neighborhood in Panama City, Blades grew up listening not only to his parents' music but also to that of Elvis Presley and the Beatles. He wanted to become a musician, but his father—who was also a policeman—insisted that the young Blades attend college to study law. Blades kept up with his music by singing with local Latin bands while studying for law classes at the University of Panama. After he graduated and passed the bar (an exam allowing lawyers to practice), he became a lawyer for the Bank of Panama. He then headed to the United States for a visit.

The visit turned out to be longer than Blades had expected. While in New York City, he hovered between careers for a time, still weighing his love for music against his interest in law. The growing popularity of salsa finally won him over. *Salsa* (Spanish for "sauce") is a musical blend of various Afro-Caribbean folk styles. In the 1970s, Latin record producers in New York City began to promote the spicy dance music. After working for a while in the mailroom of Fania Records, a leading salsa label, Blades signed a contract with the company. In 1978 he and trombonist Willie Colón recorded *Siembra,* one of the best-selling salsa albums of all time.

Protest Songs Bring Danger and Success

Blades began to experiment with salsa music. He added elements of jazz and rock to the Latin beat, replacing the sound of the standard horns with that of a synthesizer. In writing his own songs, he moved away from love themes to tales of life in the barrios (Spanish neighborhoods) of New York. He borrowed ideas from his friend, Colombian novelist Gabriel García Márquez (see **Gabriel García Márquez**), and explored political issues in song. As Anthony DePalma noted in the *New York Times Magazine,* "The words [Blades] sings are not of partying, but of protest, of indignance against greed, corruption, and spiritual sloth."

Blades's resulting work stirred up controversy. In 1980 he wrote "Tiburon," a song that condemned superpowers for interfering

Rubén Blades

with the political affairs of smaller countries. Many people were outraged, interpreting the song as a direct criticism of U.S. involvement in the problems of Panama. The song was banned on Miami's Latin-music radio stations and Blades had to wear a bulletproof vest while performing there.

Despite these negative reactions, Blades's musical popularity grew. He became a leader of the *Nueva Cancion* ("New Song") movement that blended poetry and protest politics with a Latin rhythm. In an attempt to reach a larger audience, Blades signed with mainstream record company Elektra/Asylum in 1984, becoming the first Latin artist to do so. With each successive album, Blades has stretched the limits of Latin music. In the process, he has won two Grammy awards. On his albums, he has recorded duets in Spanish with such artists as Linda Ronstadt and Joe Jackson. In 1988 he surprised the Latin-music world by releasing a record in English, *Nothing but the Truth.*

Doesn't Recognize Barriers

Some Hispanics criticized Blades for abandoning his roots, but he told Guy D. Garcia of *Time* that he was open to exploring everything before him: "I refuse to acknowledge a barrier. I think the barriers are in the mind and in the heart." His desire to push through personal boundaries had become evident in 1984. That year he had put his rising musical career on hold while he studied for a master's degree in international law from Harvard University. After having completed his year-long studies, Blades changed course again and delved into acting.

In 1985 he had starred in the film *Crossover Dreams,* the story of a Latin singer who leaves his family and friends behind as he switches to mainstream music. When his efforts fail, he is left with nothing. Since that beginning, Blades has acted in several major films, including Robert Redford's *The Milagro Beanfield War* (1986), *Fatal Beauty* (1987) with Whoopi Goldberg, and *Predator II* (1991).

Blades's celebrity status has not kept him from keeping a close eye on the politics in Panama. He has been disturbed by the corruption in its government and the poor living conditions of its people. In 1989 he was critical of the United States when it invaded Panama and ousted corrupt President Manuel Noriega. With hopes of bringing democracy back to a country long ruled by dictators, Blades helped found a political party in Panama in 1991 called *Papá Egoró* ("Mother Earth" in one of Panama's native languages).

Makes a Bid for Presidency

At first, Blades did not say whether he would run for the Panamanian presidency. He told Garcia he simply hoped to create "what up to this point has been a mythical place: a Latin America that respects and loves itself, is incorruptible, romantic, nationalistic, and has a human perception of the needs of the world at large." Some Panamanian politicians, however, said Blades had no business returning to interfere in their government. In a speech reported by the Associated Press in 1993, Blades responded to his critics: "A country is not abandoned because we are far from its territory," he said, "a country is abandoned when we remove it from our heart." Later that year, he officially announced his run for the presidency.

In the months before the May 1994 election, Blades led the presidential campaign polls. But the election showed different results as Ernesto Pérez Balladares became Panama's new president. Blades came in second, receiving almost one-quarter of the vote. He returned to the United States to resume his music and film career.

For Further Information

Marton, Betty A., *Ruben Blades,* Chelsea House, 1992.
New Republic, November 1, 1993, pp. 10-11.
New York Times, March 17, 1994, p. A14; May 9, 1994, p. A4.
New York Times Magazine, June 21, 1987, pp. 24-31.
Time, January 29, 1990, pp. 70-72.

Bobby Bonilla

Professional baseball player
Born February 23, 1963, New York, New York

"There is no pressure in baseball. Pressure is growing up in the South Bronx. We're talking about houses burning and people starving...."

Bobby Bonilla

W hen he was very young, Bobby Bonilla knew that he wanted to escape the Bronx, his tough New York neighborhood. He wanted to avoid the crime, violence, and drug addiction that he saw all around him. With a little luck, the help of his family and friends, and a lot of talent, Bonilla escaped from his neighborhood into major league baseball.

Born in 1963, Bonilla was one of four children of Roberto and Regina Bonilla. While raising the family, his mother worked on a college degree in social work. His father was an electrician who sometimes took his young son with him on jobs. "My father would go up into these old buildings where the wires all look the same, so you couldn't tell negative from positive," Bonilla told Bruce Newman of *Sports Illustrated.* "Sometimes he'd get knocked off the ladder by the shocks, but he always got right back up there."

Even though Bonilla's parents divorced when he was eight, his father kept worrying about his children's welfare. By nine o'clock each night, the elder Bonilla would drive by their house and honk his horn. The Bonilla children had to wave from the windows to reassure him that they were all at home. His

mother kept close tabs on the children, too. Bonilla wanted to go to a vocational school, but his mother wanted him to receive a broader education. She enrolled him in a mostly white, middle-class school that took two city bus rides and nearly half an hour to reach.

Night-Time Batting Practice

Bonilla loved baseball and took his bat along everywhere. Batting practice could occur at any time. Much to the dismay of the younger brother who shared his bedroom, Bonilla actually slept with the bat. If something woke him up during the night, he'd hop up and take a couple of swings before settling back to sleep.

Although Bonilla excelled in baseball in high school, no major league team had sent

Bonilla hits a run-scoring single, helping the New York Mets defeat the Houston Astros, 1993

scouts to see him play before he graduated in 1981. "There are a lot of kids with talent in the cities," he explained to Newman, "and major league teams should be taking advantage of that. Maybe they're scared to go into the neighborhoods."

One person who had seen Bonilla play and knew what he could do was his high school coach, Joe Levine. When Levine learned that a national high school all-star team was going to tour Scandinavia during the summer of 1981, he filled out an application for the future baseball star. Bonilla was quickly accepted.

Performance in Europe Gains Attention

While playing for the all-star team, Bonilla caught the attention of a team member's father, who was connected with the Pittsburgh Pirates. When he returned from Europe, the Pirates offered him a minor league contract. After he batted only .217 his first season, Bonilla started taking classes at a technical college to learn to become a repairman in case his baseball career didn't work out. Because he was a switch hitter (batted either left- or right-handed) who showed promise, however, the Pirates gave him several seasons in the minors to work on his skills.

In 1985, during spring training, Bonilla broke his right leg in a collision with another player. Even though he recovered after four months, he was sent to the Pirates' lowest minor league team. When the Pirates failed to place him on their protected roster that winter, the Chicago White Sox picked him up. Four months later Pittsburgh gained him back in a trade.

Bonilla spent four seasons as a Pirate, racking up impressive statistics, collecting awards and honors, and helping the team win two divisional titles. He was named to the National League All-Star Team in 1988 and 1989. Bonilla also led National League third basemen in double plays for 1989. He finished the 1991 season among the top five hitters in eight offensive categories and was seventh in RBIs (runs-batted-in) with 100.

Signs Richest Baseball Contract

In 1992, after having become a free agent, Bonilla returned to his hometown of New York as the highest-paid professional baseball player. He signed a five-year, $29 million contract with the New York Mets. "New York City was in my heart," Bonilla told a reporter for *Jet.* "I was born and raised there. The Mets showed an interest and I said this could be a lot of fun. It'll be hard to knock the smile off my face."

However, Bonilla's first season with the Mets was disappointing. The team finished fifth in the National League East and the players were criticized by sportswriters for collecting high salaries and delivering poor performances. Bonilla improved his record in 1993 with 87 RBIs and a career-best 34 home runs, but sat out the end of the season with a shoulder injury.

In 1994 the New York Mets started a rebuilding program, trading many older players and bringing up younger ones. Bonilla became one of the leaders on the team. Bouncing back from his shoulder injury, he put together a solid season. Before the players' strike ended the baseball season early in August, Bonilla was hitting almost .300.

For Further Information

Jet, December 23, 1991, p. 46.

Knapp, Ron, *Sports Great Bobby Bonilla,* Enslow, 1993.

Rappoport, Ken, *Bobby Bonilla,* Walker and Co., 1993.

Sports Illustrated, October 14, 1991, pp. 34-41.

Alvar Núñez Cabeza de Vaca

Spanish explorer, writer
Born c. 1490, Jerez de la Frontera, Spain
Died c. 1560, Seville, Spain

"Cabeza de Vaca was one of the few Spanish explorers who managed to befriend American Indians and live among them in peace."

The remarkable life of Alvar Núñez Cabeza de Vaca was filled with action, excitement, fame, danger, courage, and hardship. He survived shipwrecks, attacks by hostile Native Americans, and grave illness in the New World. He then wrote an account of his adventures so future generations would understand the origins of the Spanish in the New World. Cabeza de Vaca was one of the few Spanish explorers who managed to befriend American Indians and live among them in peace.

Cabeza de Vaca was born around 1490 into a noble Spanish family whose name means "head of a cow" in English. In the early thirteenth century, one of his ancestors helped King Sancho of Navarre (an ancient kingdom in northern Spain) win a battle by finding a secret route through enemy lines. The ancestor, who was a shepherd, marked the road for the king's soldiers with the skull of a cow. In gratitude, the king made him a nobleman and gave him the name Cabeza de Vaca.

Little is known about Cabeza de Vaca's early life. The oldest of four children, he was raised by his grandfather in the Canary Islands (off the northwest coast of Africa). In 1511 he became a soldier and fought with the Spanish army in Spain and in Italy. He was a big, strong man with a red beard. It is believed that he married, but there is no record of his wife's name or of any children.

Sails to the New World

In 1527 Cabeza de Vaca was named royal treasurer of an expedition sent to settle and seek gold in Florida. Commanded by Pánfilo de Narváez, the expedition set out across the Atlantic Ocean with an army of six hundred men in five small ships. The ships stopped in Santo Domingo, where about 140 men deserted to live on the island. Narváez and the remaining men then spent the winter in Cuba. In April of 1528 Narváez finally landed on the shores of what is now Tampa Bay, Florida. There he took possession of the land originally claimed by Spanish explorer Juan Ponce de León (see **Juan Ponce de León**).

Native Americans in the area were not pleased to see the Spanish. Earlier goldhungry explorers had already made a poor impression through their cruelty and greed. The Native Americans directed Narváez to travel north to a place called Apalachen (present-day site of Tallahassee) to find gold.

Narváez decided to march inland toward Apalachen, taking some 300 soldiers with him, including Cabeza de Vaca. He directed the remaining soldiers to sail north along the unknown coastline and meet him in about a year. The ships were never seen again. It was later learned that they had searched in vain for Narváez before finally giving up and sailing to Mexico.

In the meantime, Narváez and his men trudged through swamps and forests for two months until they reached Apalachen. There they discovered no gold—only a small, poor village of unfriendly Native Americans who pelted them with arrows. Discouraged and hungry, the Spaniards moved on into the Florida panhandle to find food, to escape the Native Americans, and to await their ships.

Undertakes Desperate Voyage

When the Spanish ships never appeared, Narváez became desperate. He had lost many soldiers to starvation, Native American attacks, and illness. He decided to build boats to take his men back to the safety of Cuba or Mexico. None of the men were shipbuilders and no proper materials were available, but the explorers improvised to construct five seaworthy barges. Cabeza de Vaca described the process in his later account: "From the tails and manes of the horses, we made ropes and rigging, from our shirts, sails; and from the junipers growing there we made the oars."

While they were building the ships, forty men died of hunger and illness. When they hunted inland for food, Native Americans attacked. Desperate, the Spaniards were forced to kill and eat their horses, one at a time. After the last horse was slaughtered, 242 men set out to sea in their crude boats in 1528. They sailed west, trying to keep close to shore. They suffered terribly from a lack of fresh water.

After six weeks, winds and a strong current separated the boats. Cabeza de Vaca's barge was cast ashore on present-day Galveston Island, off the southeast coast of Texas. One more boat joined his group a few days later. The others were lost at sea. Only 80 explorers now remained—the first Europeans to set foot in Texas. The Native Americans who greeted them were friendly, but had little food to share with the ragged Spaniards. After a difficult winter on the island, only 15 Spanish explorers survived. The Spanish named the island *La Isla de Mal Hado* ("The Island of Bad Luck"). In the spring, 14 Spaniards left for the Texas mainland. Cabeza de Vaca, who was ill, stayed behind.

Treated as a Medicine Man by Native Americans

Cabeza de Vaca later traveled to the mainland. For several years he lived among the Native Americans. At first he was their

Cabeza de Vaca

captive. He then became a trader who traveled among several tribes along the coast. Luckily, the Native Americans considered him to be a medicine man (healer), so he was respected and was allowed to travel freely. During his travels, he became the first European to see the North American bison, or buffalo.

In 1533 Cabeza de Vaca came upon three other Spanish survivors—Alonso de Castillo, Andres Dorantes, and their Muslim slave Estevanico. They had been living as slaves with another tribe of Native Americans. The four men realized they were the only survivors out of Narváez's original group of hundreds. They agreed to attempt an escape the following summer when the tribes gathered to harvest prickly pears (fruit from the cactus of the same name).

In 1534 the four men managed to meet and break away, traveling north and west. Using diplomacy and their reputations as medicine men, the Spaniards traveled from one tribe of Native Americans to the next. They maintained the good will of all. The men moved on through Texas, into present-day New Mexico, and possibly into present-day Arizona before heading south into Mexico.

Eight-Year Journey Ends

In 1536 the four weary travelers finally came out of the wilderness and encountered a band of surprised Spanish soldiers in western Mexico. The soldiers guided them to civilization in Mexico City, where the four men were greeted as heroes and warmly welcomed by the Spanish inhabitants. The men's tales of Indian customs, enslavement, shipwreck, and survival excited the city. The explorers calculated that their eight-year journey had taken them across six thousand miles of land and water since their arrival in Florida in 1528. Cabeza de Vaca found it was difficult to adjust to city life after so much time in the wilderness. "I could not wear any [clothes] for some time," he later wrote, "nor could we sleep anywhere but on the ground."

The explorers submitted a report on their travels, which led to further expeditions, headed by Franciscan friar Marcos de Niza and explorer Francisco Vasquez de Coronado (see **Francisco Vasquez de Coronado**). Cabeza de Vaca left for Spain in 1537 to write his own account of the adventure. The finished book was titled *Relacion de los Naufragios* ("The Story of the Shipwrecked Ones").

However, this was not the end of Cabeza de Vaca's travels. In 1540 he was named governor of Spanish settlements on the Río de la Plata in the present-day South American country of Paraguay. Once again he sailed across the ocean, this time landing in Brazil, South America. He marched overland with 280 men to his post at Asunción, bartering with native people along the way for survival.

Cabeza de Vaca made a good name for himself through his honest dealings with the native people of the region. However, he angered some Spanish for neglecting what they considered to be his duty as a conqueror. In 1544 he was thrown out of his office as governor. He was then sent to Spain to be tried on a variety of charges, including the claim that he tried to subvert the authority of the king. The trial dragged on for years. Although he was found guilty, his punishment was lightened by the king. In spite of his many accomplishments and the wealth of information that he passed along to Europeans, Cabeza de Vaca spent his final years in poverty.

For Further Information

Syme, Ronald, *First Man to Cross America: The Story of Cabeza de Vaca,* Morrow, 1961.

Terrell, John Upton, *Journey Into Darkness,* Morrow, 1962.

Wojciechowska, Maia, *Odyssey of Courage,* Athenium, 1965.

José Canseco

Professional baseball player
Born July 2, 1964, Havana, Cuba

"Maybe I've learned how to handle failure. God knows, I've had my failures. But it's getting better every day. I never thought it could."

J osé Canseco, outfielder for the Texas Rangers and home run-hitting star, has been a dominating force in baseball since his debut with the Oakland Athletics in 1986. He helped the A's earn back-to-back

José Canseco

pennants and was a guiding force in the team's World Series victory in 1989. Unfortunately, Canseco's battles off the field have been equally famous. He has had run-ins with the media and the law. He has been troubled by rumors of steroid drug use—which were never proven—and some of his teammates have accused him of being distant and cold. Wherever he goes, however, fans rush to his side to meet a man many consider to be one of the best players the game of baseball has ever seen.

Canseco and his identical twin brother Osvaldo (Ozzie) were born in Cuba in 1964 to Barbara Capaz and José Canseco, Sr. The elder Canseco had been an oil company executive, but lost his job, house, and car when the communist government of Fidel Castro seized control of Cuba in 1959. Finally given permission to leave the island nation in late 1965, the Canseco family settled in Opa-Locka, Florida, northwest of Miami. To support the family, Canseco's father worked as a gas station attendant during the day and as a security guard at night.

The young Canseco did not begin to play baseball until he was ten years old, preferring instead to play soccer and basketball. In school he took his studies seriously and was a straight-A honor student through junior high school (to this day, his favorite magazine is *National Geographic* and his favorite television programs are PBS documentaries on wildlife).

Accused of Steroid Abuse

In high school Canseco was a good, but not great, baseball player. At five-foot-eleven and 165 pounds, he was considered too small to make the majors, and most team scouts thought he had reached his growth peak at seventeen. However, his powerful hitting caught the eye of a scout for the Oakland Athletics, and the team offered him a minor league contract in 1982. Over the next three years, due to rigorous weight training, Canseco put on forty pounds; he also grew four inches. Some say this phenomenal growth was from steroid drug use, but Canseco, who doesn't drink alcohol or smoke, has denied the drug charges.

After having played in the minor leagues for several years, Canseco was brought up to the Athletics' major league club in 1986. He impressed the fans almost immediately with his good looks and exciting plays. After a great season with 33 home runs, 117 runs-batted-in, and 15 stolen bases, Canseco was named the American League's Rookie of the Year. He was not a favorite with sports reporters, however. Despite the prodding of his coaches, Canseco continued to respond to reporters' questions with answers that were barely civil.

Sets Major League 40-40 Record

In 1988 the media played up Canseco's boast to hit forty home runs and steal forty bases in a single season. That feat had never been accomplished before in major league baseball, and few thought Canseco likely to set the record. Much to everyone's surprise, however, Canseco's boast proved prophetic. He finished the 1988 season with 42 home runs (including a World Series grand slam), 124 runs-batted-in, and 40 stolen bases. For his record-breaking performance, he was given the American League's Most Valuable Player award. Then his troubles began.

During the off-season between 1988 and 1989, Canseco's personal life began to make the news. He was arrested in Miami for driving 120 miles per hour. He was arrested on the campus of the University of California at San Francisco for carrying a loaded semiautomatic pistol. He cut short, or even failed to show up at, appearances at several baseball card shows and award banquets. In October 1988 he married Esther Haddad (a Miss Miami beauty queen). Over the next four-and-a-half years, the couple had a stormy relationship. Canseco filed for divorce in 1991. Even though the divorce was granted in 1992, the couple had an on-again, off-again relationship until early 1993.

A bad wrist injury at the start of the 1989 season sidelined Canseco for several months. When he recovered, his 16 home runs and 52 runs-batted-in helped the Athletics advance to their second World Series appearance in two years. This time the A's won, beating the San Francisco Giants in a series that began with an unforgettable, frightening earthquake that rumbled the stadium.

Trade Surprises Everyone

Near the end of the 1992 season, the Oakland A's surprised the sports world by trading Canseco to the Texas Rangers in exchange for three players. Canseco, who had hit 44 home runs and had driven in 122 runs during the 1991 season, was surprised as well. "I still can't believe all of this happened," he told Leigh Montville in *Sports Illustrated.* "I can't believe it happened this way." Even though he had been plagued by back and shoulder injuries all season and had barely hit .250, he did not believe his

career was over. He vowed to work hard during the off-season to regain his strength.

Although Canseco did come back, his 1993 season was marked by two embarrassing events. In May, while playing the outfield, he let a fly ball bounce off the top of his head and over the fence for a home run. That same month, he convinced his manager to let him pitch an inning against the Boston Red Sox. After throwing 33 pitches, he tore a ligament in his right elbow. He had surgery on the elbow in July and sat out the remainder of the season. Many believed his career had indeed come to an end.

At the beginning of the 1994 season, however, Canseco was healthy and optimistic. "Maybe I've learned how to handle failure," he told Richard Hoffer of *Sports Illustrated.* "God knows, I've had my failures. But it's getting better every day. I never thought it could." As the Rangers DH (designated hitter) that season, Canseco proved he was getting better. Before the season came to an early end in August because of the players' strike, Canseco had hit 31 home runs and had batted in 90 runs. Rangers manager Kevin Kennedy believed Canseco's change in attitude helped his performance. "He wants to be one of the best players in the game again," he told Jack Curry of the *New York Times.* "He wants to be the old José again."

For Further Information

Hispanic, April 1989, pp. 28-31.
New York Times, June 7, 1994, p. B11.
Sports Illustrated, August 20, 1990, pp. 42-50; September 14, 1992, pp. 36-37; March 14, 1994, pp. 38-40.

Luisa Capetillo

Feminist, labor leader, author
Born October 28, 1879, Arecibo, Puerto Rico
Died April 10, 1922, Río Piedras, Puerto Rico

"Capetillo was a tireless feminist who battled a culture that denied women educational opportunities, career choices, and economic advancement."

L uisa Capetillo was a leader in the political and labor struggles in Puerto Rico at the beginning of the twentieth century. She was also a tireless feminist who battled a culture that denied women educational opportunities, career choices, and economic advancement. Capetillo criticized a society that forced girls into marriages based not on love but on a financial agreement between parents. Many of her ideas were far ahead of her time, and she was overlooked as an important historical figure until recently.

Capetillo was born on October 28, 1879, in Arecibo, Puerto Rico. Her mother, Margarita Peron, was French, and her father, Luis Capetillo, was Spanish. She may have had some formal schooling, but she was mostly self-taught. Because she had learned French from her mother, she was able to study the works of French writers by herself.

Achieving knowledge on her own probably led to the growth of Capetillo's independent spirit in adulthood. History remembers her as the first woman to wear pants—instead of skirts or dresses—in public. Dressing in pants, like the men of the times, was a symbolic statement of Capetillo's personal freedom.

Fights for Workers' Rights

Capetillo lived in the period when industry was just beginning to develop in Puerto Rico. Although wages for men were extremely low, those for women were even lower. Capetillo believed that fair pay was a worker's right, regardless of gender. She felt that better wages for everyone would result in happier families, less domestic violence, and more educational opportunities for children.

Capetillo's main concern lay with the plight of working women. In 1911 she wrote a book called *Mi opinión sobre las libertades, derechos y deberes de la mujer como compañera, madre y ser independiente* ("My Opinion on the Freedom, Rights, and Duties of the Woman as Companion, Mother, and as an Independent Woman"). In this book she highlights the vast differences between the lives of wealthy women and the lives of working women in the early twentieth century. Wealthy women were not obligated to take jobs outside the home to help support their families; in addition, they had the financial resources to hire other women to look after their children. Capetillo's book makes clear that working women in the early 1900s did not have these luxuries but, rather, were victims of substandard economic and social conditions.

Arrested for Union Activities

Capetillo first became involved in the labor movement in 1907, when she took part in a strike in her city's tobacco factories. She was active in the local union, the Federation of Free Workers, and served as a reporter for the union's newspaper. Three years later she founded her own newspaper, *La Mujer* ("The Woman"), to bring attention to women's issues.

During the next few years Capetillo traveled quite a bit, promoting workers' rights. She journeyed to New York to write articles for a newspaper called *Cultura obrera* ("Workers' Culture"). She also met with union leaders in Florida. From 1914 to 1916 she lived in Cuba, teaching workers how to start cooperatives. (A cooperative is a group that combines its members' money or talents to buy things or to accomplish specific goals).

In 1918 Capetillo returned to Puerto Rico and immediately helped organize strikes by farm workers. That same year she was arrested for violence, disobedience, and being disrespectful to a police officer. At the time, activist-type agitation by a woman was considered shocking.

Writings Reveal Forward-Looking Beliefs

Capetillo left behind many written works that are just now being rediscovered and studied. Dedicated to all workers, her essays and books reveal her dreams of a better world in the future. In *La humanidad en el futuro* ("Humanity in the Future"), published in 1910, she writes about a utopian society (a perfect society governed by ideal laws), the power of the church and the state, private and public property, and marriage. Her 1911 book about women and economics analyzes gender roles in society and suggests that, through education, women can overcome the restrictions society places on them. But Capetillo did not limit her ideas to political or social essays. She also wrote several dramas. The theater gave her a chance to creatively and publicly express her radical opinions about the social oppression of women.

Capetillo died of tuberculosis on April 10, 1922, at the age of 42. She was survived by her three children, her feminist writings, and her hopes for a better world.

For Further Information

Capetillo, Luisa, *Mi opinión sobre las libertades, derechos y deberes de la mujer como compañera, madre y ser independiente* (title means "My Opinion on the Freedom, Rights, and Duties of the Woman as Companion, Mother, and as an Independent Woman"), Tomes Publishing Company, 1911.

López Antonetty, Evelina, *Luisa Capetillo*, Centro de Estudios Puertorriqueños (Hunter College), 1986.

Valle Ferrer, Norma, *Luisa Capetillo: Historia de una mujer proscrita* (title means "Luisa Capetillo: History of an Exiled Woman"), Editorial Cultural, 1990.

Lynda Cordoba Carter

Actress
Born July 24, 1951?, Phoenix, Arizona

"[My mother] taught me more than anything to survive in a dignified, honorable, gracious way."

L ynda Carter became famous by portraying Wonder Woman on television during the 1970s. The role of a superhero was appropriate for a girl from humble beginnings whose hard work and

Lynda Cordoba Carter

many talents led her to success in the entertainment world and in life. During her varied career she has been a beauty queen, television star, cosmetics model, wife, and mother.

Lynda Jean Cordoba Carter was born sometime in the early 1950s in Phoenix, Arizona. Her mother, Jean Carter, was of Mexican descent; her father was of English descent. When she was ten years old, her parents divorced and her father left the family. Carter's mother raised her three children alone and supported them by working nights in a factory. Carter admired and appreciated her mother's determination and honor. "She taught me more than anything to survive in a dignified, honorable, gracious way," Carter explained to a reporter from *People*.

Carter made her acting and singing debut in a pizza parlor when she was 15. By the time she was 17, she was singing and dancing in nightclubs in Reno and Las Vegas, Nevada. After she graduated from high school, she attended Arizona State University. Her academic

career came to an end when she won the Miss World-U.S.A. title in 1973. After her reign as a beauty queen, she studied acting. In 1975 she won the role that would make her famous: Diana Prince/Wonder Woman in the television series *Wonder Woman.*

Portrays Feminist Superhero

The strikingly beautiful 25-year-old won thousands of fans when she first appeared as the superpowered Wonder Woman. Costumed in shiny red boots, a red-white-and-blue body suit, and a gold headband and bracelet, Carter portrayed the feminist superhero for four years. During this time, she also appeared in television movies and specials, and portrayed the character of Bobbie Jo James in the 1976 motion picture *Bobbie Jo and the Outlaw.*

After her *Wonder Woman* series ended in 1979, Carter continued to act in made-for-television movies. One movie role that received a great deal of attention was her 1983 portrayal of acting legend Rita Hayworth in *Rita Hayworth: The Love Goddess.* While some friends of Hayworth did not want details of her life televised, others thought Carter was the wrong actress to play the part of the screen legend. She disagreed. "I really wanted the challenge," Carter explained to a reporter for *People*. "We both had Hispanic backgrounds. We were both in show business at an early age. We both sing and dance."

Earns Awards for Television Work

During the early 1980s Carter also appeared in her own highly rated television specials. For her 1984 special, *Linda Carter: Body and Soul,* she was nominated for an Emmy Award. In 1986 Carter was presented with the Golden Eagle Award for Consistent Performance in Television and Film.

A versatile performer, Carter also managed a career as a singer/dancer. She developed a nightclub act that originally played in Reno and Las Vegas. She then took her act around the world, performing in cities such as London, England, Monte Carlo, Monaco, and Mexico City, Mexico.

Carter has also been seen in fashion magazines as a model for Maybelline cosmetics. In addition, she served as a beauty and fashion director for Maybelline. Within two years after she signed on with the company, sales of its products tripled. A sharp businesswoman, Carter also founded her own company, Lynda Carter Productions, which continues to produce television programs.

Faces Controversy in Personal Life

Not all Carter's ventures have been successful. Her first marriage, to her talent agent, ended in divorce in 1982. She blamed the failure of the marriage on the fact that it was based on business. In 1984 she married Robert Altman, a banker. They have two children, a son, Jamie, and a daughter, Jessica. In 1991 Altman was accused of being involved in a financial scandal surrounding the vast Bank of Credit and Commerce International. While Altman had to resign from his job and defend himself, Carter insisted he was innocent. The bad publicity generated by the case often made life difficult for the couple, but Carter remained

optimistic. "This is just another challenge in my life," she told Paula Chin of *People,* "and nothing is going to derail us." In 1993 a New York jury found Altman innocent of all charges in the case.

Despite her busy personal and professional lives, Carter finds time to help others. She served as the American Cancer Society's national crusade chairperson in 1985 and 1986, and was the honorary chairperson for the Exceptional Children's Foundation in 1987 and 1988. She was also an active member of the National Committee for Arts for the Handicapped, Feed the Hungry, and the Committee for Creative Nonviolence.

For Further Information

Contemporary Theater, Film, and Television, Volume 5, Gale Research, 1988, pp. 49-50.
People, November 7, 1983, p. 109; March 19, 1984, p. 9; October 15, 1984, p. 11; February 9, 1987, p. 7; September 2, 1991, pp. 58-59.

Pablo Casals

Cellist, conductor, composer
Born December 29, 1876, Vendrell, Catalonia, Spain
Died October 22, 1973, San Juan, Puerto Rico

"The pursuit of music and the love for my neighbors have been inseparable with me, and if the first has brought me the purest and most exalted joys, the second has brought me peace of mind, even in the saddest moments."

Pablo Casals

Pablo Casals was a master musician with three loves: God, the wonders of nature, and the music of Johann Sebastian Bach. He believed the beauty found in these three could reach beyond the different languages and borders of countries, and he tried to use his music to draw humanity together in peace. When injustice and conflict among people continued, Casals responded by silencing his music.

Casals was born in 1876 in the Spanish seaside town of Vendrell. He was the son of Pilar Ursula Defilló and Carlos Casals, the local church organist and choirmaster. From the very beginning of his life, Casals was surrounded by music. As his father practiced the piano, the infant Casals would rest his head against the instrument and sing along

to the music he felt. By the age of four, Casals was playing the piano. The following year he joined the church choir. At age six he was composing songs with his father, and at nine he could play the violin and organ.

Casals was thoughtful and sensitive even as a child. From the age of ten, he began each day with a walk outdoors to find inspiration from nature. Upon returning home he would always play some of the music of Bach on his piano. He claimed this routine filled him "with an awareness of the wonder of life, with the incredible marvel of being a human being," he related to Albert E. Kahn in the book *Joys and Sorrows: Reflections by Pablo Casals as Told to Albert E. Kahn.*

Develops Unusual Cello Technique

When he was 11, Casals decided to study the cello after hearing the instrument in a chamber music recital. Although his father wanted him to apprentice to a carpenter, his mother insisted he follow his interest in music. She enrolled him in the Municipal School of Music in Barcelona, Spain.

Learning the cello quickly, Casals soon disagreed with his instructors about cello technique. He preferred to bow and finger the instrument in his own style. His experiments produced a range of sound that was considered unusually expressive. Many thought his style was revolutionary and credited Casals with elevating the cello to a higher position as a solo instrument.

Casals's reputation spread quickly. In 1894, at age 18, he was invited to perform informal concerts for the Queen Regent of Spain, Maria Cristine. During the next few years he played with orchestras in Paris and

Madrid. In 1899 he made his formal debut as a concert soloist with the prestigious orchestra of French conductor Charles Lamoureux. What audiences heard in his playing was a reverence for the world around him. This was especially evident in his interpretation of the music of Bach.

Brings New Light to the Music of Bach

Sometime in 1890, while browsing through a Barcelona bookstore, Casals had found a volume of Bach's Six Suites for solo cello. The discovery had been enlightening. These suites had always been considered mere musical exercises, but Casals saw something deeper and richer in them. He practiced the suites every day for 12 years before playing them in public. He continued to play at least one suite every day for the rest of his life. Casals's performance of Bach's suites astounded listeners and made the music world take a new look at these compositions. While many thought Bach's solo music for strings had no warmth or artistic value, Casals showed that Bach was "a fully human creator whose art had poetry and passion, accessible to all people," H. L. Kirk wrote in *Pablo Casals: A Biography.*

While Casals had been in school, he came to understand the suffering and inequality of humankind as he walked among the poor on the streets of Barcelona. He vowed to use his gift from God—his music—for the welfare of others. "The pursuit of music and the love for my neighbors have been inseparable with me," he related to José Maria Corredor in the book *Conversations With Casals,* "and if the first has brought me the purest and most exalted joys, the second has brought me

peace of mind, even in the saddest moments." Throughout his career Casals helped the disadvantaged by writing letters and organizing concerts. He also refused to perform in countries whose governments he considered unjust.

During the Spanish Civil War in the 1930s, Casals supported the Republican cause. When Nationalist General Francisco Franco seized control of the government in 1939, Casals left Spain, announcing he would never return until Franco was removed. He settled in Prades, France, giving occasional concerts until 1946. That year, as a further protest against military dictatorships around the world, Casals vowed never to perform again. A peaceful man, he believed his silence was the loudest, strongest protest he could make.

Four Years of Silence

Casals did not play his cello in public again until 1950, when friends persuaded him to participate in a musical festival celebrating the two hundredth anniversary of Bach's death. Even though he performed, Casals did not abandon his cause. At the end of every concert he gave, Casals played his arrangement of a Spanish folk ballad, "Song of the Birds," to protest the oppressive government in Spain.

Casals never returned to Spain. In 1956 he settled in Puerto Rico, his mother's homeland. He started the world-famous Casals Festival to spur artistic and cultural activities on the island. With his help, a symphony orchestra and a conservatory of music were also organized there.

Although Casals resumed performing, he refused to play in any country that officially recognized the Franco government in Spain. The United States was one of these countries. He wavered from that decision only once, in 1961. U.S. President John F. Kennedy, a man Casals greatly admired, asked him to perform at the White House and Casals agreed.

Throughout his life, Casals was inspired by the beauty he found in nature and in music. Through both his cello and his silence, he sought to promote harmony among people. At Casals's funeral in 1973, his recording of "The Song of the Birds" was played as his last poignant plea for peace in the world.

For Further Information

Casals, Pablo, *Song of the Birds: Sayings, Stories, and Impressions of Pablo Casals,* Robsons Books, 1985.

Casals, Pablo, and Albert E. Kahn, *Joys and Sorrows: Reflections by Pablo Casals as Told to Albert E. Kahn,* Simon and Schuster, 1970.

Corredor, José Maria, *Conversations With Casals,* Hutchinson, 1956.

Garza, Hedda, *Pablo Casals,* Chelsea House, 1993.

Kirk, H. L., *Pablo Casals: A Biography,* Holt, Rinehart, Winston, 1974.

Rosemary Casals

Professional tennis player
Born September 16, 1948, San Francisco,
California

"The other kids had nice tennis clothes, nice rackets, nice white shoes, and came in Cadillacs. I felt stigmatized because we were poor."

osemary Casals earned her reputation as a rebel in the staid tennis world when she began competing in the early 1960s. During a tennis career that spanned more than two decades, she won more than 90 tournaments and worked for the betterment of women's tennis. She was a motivating force behind many of the changes that shook the tennis world during the 1960s and 1970s. Many of these changes helped make tennis the popular sport that it is today.

Casals was born in 1948 in San Francisco, California, to poor parents who had immigrated to the United States from the Central American country of El Salvador. Less than a year after Casals was born, her parents decided they could not care for her and her older sister Victoria. Casals's great-uncle and great-aunt, Manuel and Maria Casals, then took the young girls in and raised them as their own. When the children grew older, Manuel Casals took them to the public tennis courts of San Francisco and taught them how to play the game. He became the only coach Casals would ever have.

While still just a teenager, Casals began to rebel on the court. She hated the tradition of younger players competing only against each other on the junior circuit. Gutsy and determined right from the start, Casals wanted to work as hard as possible to better her game. For an added challenge, she often entered tournaments to play against girls who were two or three years older.

Set Apart by Height and Class

Junior tennis was the first of several obstacles Casals faced during her tennis career.

At five-feet-two-inches tall, she was one of the shortest players on the court. Another disadvantage for her was class distinction. Traditionally, tennis was a sport practiced in expensive country clubs by the white upper class. Casals's ethnic heritage and poor background immediately set her apart from most of the other players. "The other kids had nice tennis clothes, nice rackets, nice white shoes, and came in Cadillacs," Casals related to a reporter for *People*. "I felt stigmatized because we were poor."

Unfamiliarity with country club manners also made Casals feel different from the other players. Traditionally, audiences applauded only politely during matches and players wore only white clothes on the court. Both of these practices seemed foolish to Casals. She believed in working hard to perfect her game and expected the crowd to show its appreciation for her extra efforts. In one of her first appearances at the tradition-filled courts at Wimbledon, England—site of the British tennis championships—she was nearly excluded from competition for not wearing white. Later in her career, she became known for her brightly-colored outfits.

Wins with Aggressive Style

The frustrations Casals endured due to her size and background affected her playing style. Despite her sweet-sounding nicknames, "Rosie" and "Rosebud," she was known as a determined player who used any shot avaliable to her to score a point—even one between her legs. "I wanted to *be* someone," Casals was quoted as saying in Alida M. Thacher's *Raising a Racket: Rosie Casals*. "I knew I was good, and winning tournaments—it's a kind of way of being ac-

Rosemary Casals

cepted." By age 16 Casals was the top junior and women's-level player in northern California. At 17 she was ranked eleventh in the country and was earning standing ovations for her aggressive playing style.

More experience on the national and international levels of play helped Casals improve her game. In 1966 she and Billie Jean King, her doubles partner, won the U.S. hardcourt and indoor tournaments. That same year they reached the quarterfinals in the women's doubles at Wimbledon. In 1967 Casals and King took the doubles crown at Wimbledon and at the United States and South African championships. The two dominated women's doubles play for years, becoming one of the most successful duos in tennis history. (They are the only doubles team to have won U.S. titles on grass, clay, indoor, and hard surfaces.) Casals was also a successful individual player, ranking third among U.S. women during this period.

Fights for Rights of Professional and Women Players

Despite her victories on the courts, Casals continued to fight tennis traditions on several fronts. Amateur tennis players (those who are unpaid) had always been favored over professionals (those who were paid). Because many tennis players came from non-wealthy backgrounds, they were forced to accept money in order to continue playing. This, in turn, made them professionals and prevented them from entering major tournaments that allowed only amateurs to play, such as Wimbledon. Fighting against this discrimination, Casals worked for an arrangement that allowed both amateur and professional tennis players to compete in the same tournaments.

Casals's next challenge was to overcome the vast difference in prize monies awarded to male and female players. Even though they worked just as hard and played just as often as men, women earned much smaller prizes. In 1970 Casals and other women threatened to boycott traditional tournaments if they were not paid higher prize money and not given more media attention. The ruling body of U.S. tennis, the United States Lawn Tennis Association (USLTA), refused to listen to their demands. In response, the women established their own tournament, the Virginia Slims Invitational.

The attention generated by this successful tournament quickly brought about the formation of other women's tournaments and greater prize monies for women.

Casals soon became involved in another innovation: World Team Tennis (WTT). WTT involved tennis teams, each made up of two women and four men, from cities throughout the United States. Matches included both singles and doubles games. During her years with WTT, Casals played with the Detroit Loves and the Oakland Breakers and coached the Los Angeles Strings.

The strain of playing almost constantly took a physical toll on Casals. She underwent knee surgery in 1978 and was forced to change career directions. Since 1981 she has been president of Sportswomen, Inc., a California company she formed to promote a Women's Classic tour for older female players. She also began the Midnight Productions television company and has broadened her own sporting activities to include golf. Casals continues to search for new chances to improve the game of tennis. In 1990, she again teamed with Billie Jean King to win the U.S. Open Seniors' women's doubles championship.

For Further Information

Jacobs, Linda, *Rosemary Casals: The Rebel Rosebud,* EMC Corporation, 1975.
People, May 31, 1982, p. 85.
Thacher, Alida M., *Raising a Racket: Rosie Casals,* Children's Press, 1976.

Sylvia L. Castillo

Founder, National Network of Hispanic Women
Born September 2, 1951, Los Angeles, California

"The more isolated we stay as women, the less opportunity we have."

Sylvia L. Castillo is a clinical social worker who has led the call for greater communication and support among Hispanic professional women across the country. In the 1980s she cofounded the National Network of Hispanic Women and its English-language magazine, *Intercambios,* to inspire young Hispanic women to pursue higher education and challenging careers. For her work she has been honored by the United Nations Council on Women and the California State Assembly.

Castillo was born in 1951 in Los Angeles, California. Her grandparents had immigrated to the United States from Mexico. Her parents were Henry Castillo, a truck driver, and Lucille Miramontes Castillo, a pharmacy clerk who eventually worked her way up to become a medical representative for a home health care agency. Castillo's mother was an influential presence in her life, passing on the idea that opportunities arose through hard work.

Interested in Women's Mental Health

Castillo attended an all-girls parochial school (a private school run by a church or other religious organization) where she was student body president in her senior year.

After she graduated in 1969, she hoped for a career in psychology (the science of human behavior). She was especially interested in women's mental health issues. "If a mother feels good, then her daughters feel good," she related to Ann Malaspina in *Notable Hispanic American Women.* "If a mother has good self-esteem, her children will have good self-esteem."

Sylvia earned a bachelor's degree in social psychology from the University of California at Santa Barbara in 1973. Three years later she completed work on a master's degree in social welfare administration from the University of California at Berkeley. For nine years she worked as a career and mental health counselor and academic advisor at different colleges.

Newsletter Reaches Out to Professional Hispanic Women

During her years of research, Castillo began wondering what it took for a Hispanic student to succeed. To find an answer, she interviewed dozens of successful Hispanic women who worked in higher education. What she discovered, instead, was that they all shared a problem—they felt isolated. This led Castillo to focus on the difficulties faced by Hispanic professional women. To help these Hispanic women share their experiences and offer each other practical information on careers, Castillo started a newsletter, *Intercambios* ("Interchange").

Each issue of the newsletter had a theme, such as careers in science and technology or health and the Hispanic woman. *Intercambios* profiled successful Hispanic women and printed the latest studies done on Hispanics and their culture. Controversial topics such as affirmative action were also explored.

Intercambios proved popular and led to the development of the National Network of Hispanic Women (NNHW), an organization of Hispanic women dedicated to educational, career, and leadership development. Castillo worked without pay to recruit a board of advisors to help launch the group. She asked a wide range of Hispanic teachers, bankers, scientists, businesspeople, and community activists for support and advice. NNHW quickly began its work of drawing Hispanic women together to improve their professional opportunities. By the mid-1980s the Network had some 500 members and *Intercambios* had 6,500 subscribers.

Sidelined by Illness

In 1986, because of illness, Castillo was forced to resign her leadership roles in the NNHW and at *Intercambios*. During that year she married Steven Castillo Long and moved to Maui, Hawaii. Before long she was actively involved with the Puerto Rican community and with women's groups there. All the while, she kept in touch with the NNHW.

In the early 1990s the NNHW faced trouble raising enough money to continue, and Castillo returned to Los Angeles. She felt it was necessary for Hispanic women to change in order to handle the economic uncertainties of the 1990s. "As we're affected by downsizing, mergers, job loss, we're going to have to redefine success," Castillo observed, "otherwise it will be easy for the Hispanic woman to internalize that she's failed."

Castillo continues to be active with NNHW. She urges Hispanic women to make

communication with each other an important goal. As she told Malaspina, "The more isolated we stay as women, the less opportunity we have."

For Further Information

Hispanic Business, July 1988, pp. 25-26.
Hispanic USA, May 1985, pp. 14-15.
Notable Hispanic American Women, Gale Research, 1993, pp. 85-87.

Lauro Cavazos

Former U.S. secretary of education
Born January 4, 1927, King Ranch, Texas

"Education is perhaps our most serious deficit."

Lauro Cavazos's career in education has been full of ups and downs. He rose through the ranks as a teacher, principal, professor, and college president to become the U.S. secretary of education in 1988. This appointment made him the first Hispanic member of a president's cabinet (the group of advisors who are also heads of the federal government's executive departments). Shortly after his appointment by President Ronald Reagan, Cavazos told Robert Marquand of the *Christian Science Monitor,* "Education is perhaps our most serious deficit." His vision of the problems of education in America, however, were not matched by his actions on them. Highly criticized for being ineffective, Cavazos was forced to resign his position in December 1990.

Lauro Fred Cavazos, Jr., was born in 1927 at Texas's legendary King Ranch to the ranch's cattle foreman, Lauro Fred Cavazos, and his wife, Tomasa Quintanilla. Bilingualism (speaking two languages) was an issue early in Cavazos's life: while growing up he spoke Spanish to his mother and English to his father. Through the second grade he attended the ranch's two-room Hispanic elementary school. When his family left the ranch and moved to the nearby city of Kingsville, the young Cavazos attended a public school, where he became its first Hispanic student.

Education Wins out over Fishing

After high school, Cavazos enlisted in the U.S. Army. Upon his return home, he planned to become a commercial fisherman. His father, who had always stressed education, made it clear that college would come first. Cavazos turned out to have a talent for education. After first attending Texas A & I University, he transferred to Texas Tech University where he earned a bachelor's degree in zoology (the study of animals and animal life) in 1949 and a master's degree in cytology (the study of cells) in 1951. He continued his education at Iowa State University, earning a doctorate in physiology (the study of how living organisms function) in 1954.

That same year Cavazos married Peggy Ann Murdock, a registered nurse. They eventually went on to raise a family of ten children. Cavazos began teaching classes at the Medical College of Virginia and, later, at Tufts University School of Medicine in Massachusetts. In 1975 he was appointed dean of the medical school at Tufts. In 1980

Lauro Cavazos

he left Tufts to became the first Hispanic president of Texas Tech University.

Texas-Sized Controversies

While at Texas Tech, Cavazos helped improve fundraising, increased the number of minority students, and enhanced the university's research programs. He headed a committee to study the reasons for dropouts in area schools. He also visited local schools regularly, helping to increase Hispanic enrollment through his personal appearances.

Despite these achievements, Cavazos also earned his share of negative publicity while at Texas Tech. In 1984 he attempted to limit the number of professors that were granted tenure (status granted to long-serving teachers that prevents them from being fired without a proper hearing). Outraged, the faculty at the college fought his proposal. The controversy came to the attention of then-President Ronald Reagan. Approving of Cavazos's stance, the president honored him with an Outstanding Leadership Award. The argument between the Texas Tech faculty and Cavazos continued for two years until he compromised with a modified policy regarding tenure.

Another controversy marked Cavazos's term as Texas Tech's president. The school's football team was charged with violating national college rules regarding the recruitment of high school players. As a result, the team was put on a one-year probation by the National Collegiate Athletic Association.

Becomes First Hispanic in the Presidential Cabinet

In spite of the bad publicity, President Reagan nominated Cavazos for the prestigious post of U.S. secretary of education in late 1988. When fellow Republican George Bush succeeded Reagan as president the following January, he reappointed Cavazos to the post. Many people applauded the move. Cavazos had a reputation as someone who was willing to listen to and work things out with his opponents.

As the country's education leader, Cavazos promoted the same policies that concerned him in Texas. He worked to make education more easily available to the poor and to minorities. He supported bilingualism in schools. He spoke in favor of school "choice"—the idea that parents should be allowed to choose the best local school for their children. This was Cavazos's major theme, as he explained to Thomas H. Sharpe

in *Hispanic:* "The key to the primary issues of education has to be the parent.... I feel that teachers and parents should be given more responsibility for decisions they make at the school level."

Focuses Attention on Hispanic Education

Cavazos was sensitive to the educational needs of Hispanics in the United States. He brought this issue to the attention of the Congress and the president. In 1989 he helped persuade President Bush to sign an executive order creating the President's Council on Educational Excellence for Hispanic Americans. Concerned with the high dropout rate of Hispanics, Cavazos traveled extensively to encourage students to stay in school.

Many education leaders, however, were not happy with Cavazos's tenure as secretary. They believed he simply liked making appearances, which did not do enough to solve more serious educational problems. Many shared the view of *Time*'s Susan Tifft, who wrote that Cavazos "comes across as a man with no clear-cut agenda who prefers speechmaking to policymaking." Cavazos also came under fire when he was accused of breaking government travel rules by allowing his wife to accompany him on business trips and by scheduling expensive flights on an airline for which one of his children worked.

President Bush, who had made the 1988 campaign pledge to be the "education President," was also attacked for not bringing about quicker solutions to the problems in education. The controversy surrounding the secretary continued until December 1990, when Cavazos resigned his position at the Department of Education. He was replaced by Lamar Alexander, a former governor of Tennessee.

For Further Information

Christian Science Monitor, October 21, 1988.
Hispanic, May 1989, p. 32.
Time, May 29, 1989, p. 76; December 24, 1990, p. 64.
U.S. News and World Report, May 21, 1990, pp. 14-16.

César Chávez

Labor leader, founder of the United Farm
   Workers
Born March 31, 1927, Yuma, Arizona
Died April 23, 1993, San Luis, Arizona

"For most of his life, César Estrada Chávez chose to live penniless and without property, devoting everything he had, including his frail health, to the UFW."—Peter Matthiesen, New Yorker

Renowned labor leader César Estrada Chávez was raised in a poor family that lost its farm during the Depression and was forced into migrant farm labor when Chávez was only ten years old. As a boy Chávez had little time for school or leisure activities, and he frequently experienced racial prejudice because of his Mexican American heritage. Despite these obstacles, Chávez rose to become a gifted leader and organizer who inspired thousands of people to better their lives. During the 1960s he founded the United Farm Workers, an organization that led its members in the fight for improved working conditions.

Chávez was born to Librado Chávez and Juana Estrada in 1927 on the family's farm in Arizona. He was a child during the Great Depression, a period in the late 1920s and 1930s when the United States suffered from an extremely slow economy and widespread unemployment. During this time, many people lost their jobs and homes, and some were forced to wander the country in search of work. In the American Southwest, farmers were further devastated by the effects of a severe drought on their crops. They could hardly sell what they could grow, and eventually they were not able to grow anything at all.

The Chávez family fell victim to the drought. With no money coming in, Librado Chávez could not pay the taxes on their land, and the farm was lost in 1937. The Chávezes were forced to become migrant farm workers, wandering throughout Arizona and California following the harvest of other landowners' crops. Since his family never stayed in one place for very long, Chávez attended over 30 different schools and was able to achieve only a seventh grade education.

The Plight of Migrant Farm Workers

Life for migrant farm workers was incredibly difficult. They toiled in the hot sun for hours picking beans, peas, grapes, beets, cucumbers, tomatoes, cotton, and other crops. Sometimes they were paid 50 cents for every basket they picked. Other times they were paid only 20 cents. At the end of the day, some farm owners subtracted money from the laborers' pay for any water they drank while in the fields. At night, farm workers were often forced to sleep in run-down shacks or in their cars if they could not afford a room. And, since many of the migrant laborers were of Mexican or Mexican American descent and knew little English, unscrupulous farm owners often took advantage of the language barrier and swindled them out of the money they had rightfully earned for their work.

Throughout the 1930s and 1940s, Chávez and his family faced prejudice everywhere—in the schools, in the fields, in the towns. Restaurants refused to serve Mexican Americans and theaters allowed them to sit only in certain sections. In 1944, when he was 17 years old, Chávez joined the U.S. Navy to fight in World War II. Even while fighting for his country, he experienced discrimination because of his Mexican American background. After two years of service, Chávez returned to California to work on the farms. In 1948 he married Helen Fabela, settled down in a one-room shack in the town of Delano (where he picked grapes and cotton), and began to raise a family. Over the years, the couple had eight children.

The prejudices and poor working conditions facing migrant farm workers before the war did not change after it. Because of the experiences of his childhood, Chávez was greatly concerned with solving the problems of the nation's farm laborers. In 1952 he met Fred Ross, founder of the Community Service Organization (CSO), a group that sought better living conditions for migrant workers. Impressed with Ross and his ideas, Chávez began working for the CSO as a community organizer. Going from door to door at night, he helped some workers with their day-to-day problems, instructed others on how to become U.S. citizens, and encouraged all to register to vote. By 1958 Chávez had become director of the CSO in California and Arizona.

Struggles to Form a Union

Chávez heard many complaints from migrant workers as he traveled between the two states. He was especially concerned about claims that landowners often used Mexican farmhands—who were illegally bused across the U.S. border—to work in the fields for the lowest of wages. This prevented migrant workers already living in the United States from getting jobs on American farms. Since the workers were not organized as a group, however, they could not effectively protest the situation. Over the next few years, Chávez tried to convince CSO leaders to develop a special farm labor union that would work to improve the rights of migrant workers. When the CSO refused to do so, Chávez resigned from the organization in 1962.

Chávez and his family then settled down again in Delano, California, where he began to organize the National Farm Workers Association. For several years, Chávez worked 18-hour days for very little or no money at all. He drove to the fields and talked to the workers, urging them to join the National Farm Workers Association. The uneducated migrant workers were a difficult group to organize, and at times Chávez felt discouraged and defeated. But by continually pressing ahead with his efforts, he began to meet with success and the union slowly increased its ranks.

César Chávez

Huelga!

In 1965 the National Farm Workers Association was catapulted to national attention. Migrant grape pickers in Delano, who worked under harsh conditions for a dollar an hour, went on strike. They wanted the association to back them, but Chávez thought the union was still too young and weak. National Farm Workers Association members disagreed and voted to join the strike. Once the *Huelga* (Spanish for "strike") was on, Chávez worked tirelessly for the cause. The picket lines grew as more and more workers left the fields. Nonetheless, the landowners refused to give in to the workers' demands for better wages and

working conditions. Some even threatened the workers with violence.

Chávez believed in nonviolent methods of social change. He had studied the life and teachings of Mohandas Gandhi, who had helped India gain its independence from England in 1947 through nonviolent means. Chávez responded to the landowners' threats by calling for a countrywide boycott of grapes. By discouraging the American people from buying grapes until working conditions for grape pickers improved, he attracted national attention to the plight of the farm workers. Many large labor unions supported Chavez and the strikers, including the AFL-CIO (American Federation of Labor and

Congress of Industrial Organizations) and the United Auto Workers. Robert F. Kennedy, an influential senator from New York, also gave his support to the cause.

In March of 1966 the strikers marched 250 miles from Delano to the California capital of Sacramento to take their demands to state officials. By the time they arrived in Sacramento, one of several large grape companies had agreed to sign a contract with the workers. But the fight was not yet over. Soon the Teamsters Union, the powerful truckers' alliance led by Jimmy Hoffa, began to compete with the National Farm Workers Association for its members. To strengthen the association, Chávez merged his organization with part of the AFL-CIO, America's oldest and strongest group of unions. The new union was called the United Farm Workers Organizing Committee (UFWOC). After 1972 it was known simply as the United Farm Workers (UFW).

Fast Gains National Attention

The struggle against the grape growers continued throughout the late 1960s. In February of 1968, to draw more attention to the strike, Chávez began a 25-day fast, during which he ate no solid food. People across the nation sympathized with Chávez's commitment to the cause and his nonviolent means to achieve justice. The grape boycott spread and the grape companies lost money. Finally, in June of 1970, vineyard owners agreed to a contract with the UFWOC that gave workers health insurance benefits and a raise in pay.

But the celebration did not last long. Chávez quickly turned his attention to the problems of America's lettuce workers. The Teamsters Union had signed contracts with lettuce growers that hurt rather than helped migrant workers. Chávez again organized strikes and rallies, and he called for a national boycott of lettuce. The struggle against the growers and the Teamsters, which at times had turned violent, finally came to an end in 1975 when California governor Jerry Brown passed the Agricultural Labor Relations Act. This was the first bill of rights for farm workers ever enacted in the United States, and it allowed them to vote on which union would best represent their needs. In elections held in August of that year, the UFW clearly beat the Teamsters.

In the 1980s Chávez protested against grape growers who used pesticides (chemicals used to kill insects) on their crops. He believed the pesticides were dangerous not only to the farm workers who picked the grapes but also to the general public who consumed the grapes. He called for another boycott, and in 1988 he fasted for 36 days. Although his fast again gained national attention, the boycott did not take hold as earlier ones had. The fight for farm workers' rights continued.

"For most of his life," Peter Matthiessen wrote in the *New Yorker,* "César Estrada Chávez chose to live penniless and without property, devoting everything he had, including his frail health, to the UFW." While in Arizona on union business in April of 1993, Chávez died in his sleep. Messages of sympathy came from leaders of churches and government, including Pope John Paul II and U.S. president Bill Clinton. More than 30,000 mourners formed a three-mile-long funeral procession to carry Chávez's body to its final resting place. A year after Chávez died, famed playwright and director Luis Valdez (see **Luis Valdez**) began writing a script for a film biography about the late labor leader.

For Further Information

Cedeño, Maria E., *Cesar Chavez,* Millbrook, 1993.

Franchere, Ruth, *Cesar Chavez,* HarperCollins Children's Books, 1986.

New Yorker, May 7, 1993, p. 82.

Roberts, Maurice, *Cesar Chavez and La Causa,* Children's Press, 1986.

Rodriguez, Consuelo, *Cesar Chavez,* Chelsea House, 1991.

Evelyn Cisneros

Ballerina
Born 1955, Long Beach, California

"I'm proud to be able to represent my people, although I've never been through what many of them have."

Evelyn Cisneros

As principal dancer with the San Francisco Ballet Company, Evelyn Cisneros has achieved national fame. She has danced such classic ballets as *Swan Lake, Sleeping Beauty,* and *Romeo and Juliet,* as well as more modern works. Her grace, talent, and hard work have made her a role model for dancers and for other Hispanic Americans as well. In 1992 she was listed in *Hispanic Business*'s "100 Influentials."

Cisneros was born in 1955 in Long Beach, California. While growing up, she was extremely shy. To help her overcome her fears, her mother enrolled her in a ballet class. One of her teachers immediately recognized Cisneros's dancing abilities and encouraged her to study tap, jazz, and flamenco dancing as well.

Cisneros was an enthusiastic pupil who took her lessons very seriously. By the time she reached high school, she was making three-hour round-trip drives every day to her dance classes in Los Angeles. Despite the difficult and tiring schedule, she still managed to keep up with her homework.

Enters the World of Ballet

Cisneros's years of training were rewarded in 1977 when, at the age of 22, she was invited to join the San Francisco Ballet. She was such an outstanding dancer that the company's artistic director created a ballet for her just two years later. It was a tribute to Native Americans entitled *A Song for Dead Warriors.* The ballet and her performance in it were later honored by being broadcast on

Cisneros performs with Anthony Randazzo, San Francisco Ballet

the *Great Performances—Dance in America* series on public television.

A Song for Dead Warriors is a personal favorite of the ballerina for whom it was written. "I feel very special about being able to make a statement about the Indian situation in the country," Cisneros told a reporter for *Nuestro*. "I dated an Indian guy for five years. I met his family and went to powwows with him. I saw how deep the sadness goes."

During the 1980s Cisneros's fame grew. She made headlines in newspapers and was featured on the covers of *Dance Magazine* and *Ballet News*. Despite this fact, she has been content to remain with the small, regional San Francisco Ballet rather than switch to a national company. She has cited the many opportunities presented to her over the years in San Francisco as the main reason.

Performs for Her Community

In San Francisco, Cisneros has been able to reach out and help not only the area's artistic community but also its Hispanic community. In September 1991 she was selected as a godparent for the new School of Creative Arts at San Francisco State University. In 1988 she participated as a spokesperson in the Fifth Annual Chicano/Latino Youth Leadership Conference held at California State University in Hayward. "I'm proud to be able to represent my people," she told a reporter for *Nuestro,* "although I've never been through what many of them have." Cisneros has also lent her talents to many benefits, including the Children's Hospital National Telethon in June 1991.

Cisneros has made guest appearances in ballets around the world. In America she has danced behind the symphony orchestras from Detroit and Los Angeles. In Tucson, Arizona, she danced at the Heard Museum to celebrate the opening of the new American Indian Wing of the museum. In 1982 she performed *Stravinsky Piano Pieces* in a live television broadcast from the White House. Cisneros has danced with the Royal New Zealand Ballet and has performed in Mexico City, Mexico, and in Madrid, Spain. In 1984 and again in 1988 she was asked by the famed Cuban ballerina Alicia Alonso to perform at the International Ballet Festival held in Havana, Cuba.

For Further Information

Ballet News, February 1985.
Dance Magazine, December 1983; August 1988; January 1992, pp. 100-03.
Hispanic, July 1989, p. 36+.
Nuestro, August 1985.
Simon, Charnan, *Evelyn Cisneros: Prima Ballerina,* Children's Press, 1990.

Henry G. Cisneros

Secretary of U.S. Department of Housing and Urban Development, former mayor of San Antonio, Texas
Born June 11, 1947, San Antonio, Texas

"We can go four whole years wallowing in examples of absolute despair, but it's time to say to people: You can do it. We can do it. I have seen it done."

Henry G. Cisneros was the first Hispanic mayor of a prominent American city and, beginning in 1992, has served as a key member of President Bill Clinton's cabinet (a body of consultants on government policy). Well educated, charismatic, and fluent in both Spanish and English, Cisneros is often the first Hispanic spokesperson called by the media to comment on current social and political issues. While he was mayor of San Antonio, Texas, he helped forge closer ties between his city's Hispanic and Anglo (white) communities. As secretary of the U.S. Department of Housing and Urban Development (HUD), Cisneros has tried to overcome the great economic problems in the country that have left millions of people of all ethnic backgrounds in a state of poverty.

Cisneros was one of five children born in a middle-class Hispanic section of San Antonio to Elvira and George Cisneros. His family has a long history in the American Southwest. His father's ancestors were given land grants in New Mexico by the Spanish almost 300 years ago. His mother's father took part in the Mexican Revolution in the early 1900s, barely escaping to Texas with his life.

Cisneros's family was very close-knit and hardworking. No weekday television was allowed, except for the news or *National Geographic* specials. During the summers, the Cisneros children were given chores, reading assignments, and creative projects by their mother. Weekend trips to the museum, opera, and symphony were common.

Changes Career Path from Flying to Politics

Cisneros attended San Antonio's Catholic schools and was such an excellent student that he was allowed to skip the third grade. After he graduated from high school at the age of 16, he wanted to enter the U.S. Air Force Academy in Colorado to become a pilot. Because he was too young and too small to be accepted, he enrolled at Texas A&M University. He originally studied aeronautical engineering but switched to city management during his sophomore year. By the time he graduated from college in 1968, he had made up his mind that he would one day be mayor of San Antonio. The next year, he married Mary Alice Perez, whom he had met in high school.

In 1970, after having earned a master's degree in urban planning from Texas A&M, Cisneros moved to Washington, D.C. to work at various government jobs. The following year, he became the youngest person ever to be named a White House fellow (a graduate student who serves as an assistant to a member of the president's cabinet or White House staff). He served under Eliot L. Richardson, then secretary of Health, Education, and Welfare. After his fellowship ended, Cisneros attended the John F. Kennedy School of Government at Harvard University, where he earned a master's degree in public administration. In 1975 he received a doctoral degree in that field from George Washington University in Washington, D.C. He then returned to his hometown.

That same year Cisneros won a seat on San Antonio's city council, becoming the youngest councilperson in the city's history. He subsequently won two more elections, serving on the council for a total of six years. Cisneros gained a reputation as a sharp politician. He worked to strengthen the city in many ways and gained federal funds to improve living conditions in San Antonio's Hispanic sections.

Becomes Mayor of San Antonio

In 1981 Cisneros ran for mayor of the city and won. San Antonio is the ninth-largest city in the United States, and Cisneros became the first Mexican American to head a major American city. He was well-liked by his constituency and was reelected to three additional two-year terms. His popularity did not rest with San Antonio's Hispanic community alone, but with all ethnic groups in the area. Instead of asking for federal funds to improve his city, he worked to attract high-tech companies to San Antonio to provide more jobs and a better economy for everyone.

The improvements Cisneros brought to San Antonio gained national attention. In 1984 Democratic presidential candidate Walter F. Mondale seriously considered Cisneros as his running mate. The following year, Cisneros was elected to a one-year term as president of the National League of Cities.

Citizens urged Cisneros to run for governor of Texas in 1990, but a family crisis forced him to change his goals. His son, John Paul, had been born in 1987 with a heart defect. At the time, doctors did not know if surgery could correct his problem. (He finally underwent successful surgery in late 1993). His son's health became his biggest priority, and Cisneros wished to stay close to home to spend as much time as possible with his family. He also turned down an appointment as a U.S. senator from Texas in 1992.

A National Government Official

Cisneros could not, however, remain out of public service for long. Racial tensions exploded and riots erupted in Los Angeles in April of 1992 following the emotionally charged trial of white police officers accused of beating African American motorist Rodney King. In response, Cisneros immediately flew to the city and tried to calm its angry residents. That same year he worked hard on Bill Clinton's Democratic presidential campaign. After Clinton was elected president, he asked Cisneros to join his administration as the secretary of Housing and Urban Development. Since directing HUD would still allow Cisneros time to spend with his family, he accepted.

From the beginning, however, Cisneros's job at HUD was not easy. For nearly ten years prior to his appointment, HUD had been severely mismanaged. In addition, the 1980s saw a dramatic rise in the number of homeless people in the United States. Cisneros made the elimination of homelessness

Henry G. Cisneros

HUD's top priority. In addition to walking the streets of Washington, D.C.'s poorest neighborhoods at night—talking to homeless men, women, and children about their plight—he opened his agency's building on cold nights as a temporary shelter for people with no place else to go.

In addition to his struggle with housing problems, Cisneros found his public image under attack in the mid-1990s when reports appeared in the media about his involvement in an extramarital affair.

Cisneros remains frustrated that government often moves too slowly, that people continue to sleep in cardboard boxes in Washington, D.C. But within 18 months of his appointment, his tactics actually began to make a noticeable difference. Old and dangerous housing projects were torn down in cities in Washington and across the nation, and tenants were moved to better housing in better neighborhoods. Cisneros remains optimistic about the future. "We can go four whole years wallowing in examples of absolute despair," he told Lori Montgomery of the *Detroit Free Press,* "but it's time to say to people: You can do it. We can do it. I have seen it done."

For Further Information

Detroit Free Press, August 3, 1994, pp. 1A, 7A.

Diehl, Kemper, and Jan Jarboe, *Cisneros: Portrait of a New American,* Corona, 1985.

Gillies, John, *Señor Alcalde: A Biography of Henry Cisneros,* Dillon, 1988.

Martinez, Elizabeth Coonrod, *Henry Cisneros: Mexican-American Leader,* Millbrook, 1993.

U.S. News & World Report, February 21, 1994, pp. 30-31.

Sandra Cisneros

Poet, author
Born 1954, Chicago, Illinois

"It was not until this moment when I separated myself, when I considered myself truly distinct, that my writing acquired a voice."

In her poetry and stories, Mexican American author Sandra Cisneros writes about Mexican and Mexican American women who find strength to rise above the poor conditions of their lives. These types of characters have not been presented so clearly in writing before. Cisneros is determined to introduce them to American readers, and so far her efforts have been successful. A reviewer for the *Washington Post Book World* described Cisneros as "a writer of power and eloquence and great lyrical beauty."

Cisneros's ability to write about these strong characters comes from her childhood experiences. Born in Chicago, Illinois, in 1954, she grew up in poverty. As the only girl in a family of seven children, Cisneros spent a lot of time by herself. Because her family moved often, she was not able to form lasting friendships. "The moving back and forth, the new school, were very upsetting to me as a child," she explained to Jim Sagel in *Publishers Weekly.* "They caused me to be very introverted and shy. I do not remember making friends easily." Instead, Cisneros became a quiet, careful observer of the people and events around her, and recorded her feelings through secret writings at home.

Because she was too shy to volunteer or speak up in class, Cisneros often received poor grades while attending Catholic schools in Chicago. Her Mexican American mother and her Mexican father, however, both knew the importance of education. Her mother made sure all the children in the family had library cards, and her father made sure they all studied so they wouldn't have to work as hard for a living as he did. "My father's hands are thick and yellow," Cisneros wrote in *Glamour* magazine, "stubbed by a history of hammer and nails and twine and coils and springs. 'Use this' my father said, tapping his head, 'not this' showing us those hands."

Shyness Masks Her Talent

Although Cisneros learned to study hard, she was still too shy to share her creative writings at school. She felt many of her early teachers were not interested in her experiences. Finally, in the tenth grade, Cisneros was encouraged by one of her teachers to read her works to the class. She was also encouraged to work on the school's literary magazine, and eventually became its editor.

After high school, Cisneros attended Loyola University in Chicago to study English. Her father thought she might find a good husband if she went to college. What Cisneros discovered instead was the desire to be a writer. After graduating from college, encouraged by another teacher who recognized her writing talent, Cisneros enrolled in the poetry section of the Iowa Writer's Workshop, a highly respected graduate school for aspiring writers.

Cisneros's old fears about sharing her writings with others soon came back. Many of Cisneros's classmates had come from more privileged backgrounds than she had, and she felt she could not compete with them. As she explained in an interview in *Authors and Artists for Young Adults,* "It didn't take me long to learn—after a few days of being there—that nobody cared to hear what I had to say and no one listened to me even when I did speak. I became very frightened and terrified that first year."

Realizes the Importance of Her Heritage

She soon realized, however, that her experiences as a Mexican American and as a woman were very different, but just as important as anything her classmates wrote about. "It was not until this moment when I separated myself, when I considered myself truly distinct, that my writing acquired a

Sandra Cisneros

voice," she explained to Sagel. Out of this insight came her first book, *The House on Mango Street.*

Published in 1984, the book is composed of a series of connected short passages or stories told by Esperanza Cordero, a Mexican American girl growing up in a Chicago barrio (Spanish-speaking neighborhood). Much like Cisneros when she was young, Esperanza wants to leave her poor neighborhood to seek a better life for herself. As Esperanza tells her stories, readers come to understand how people live their lives in her neighborhood. Although Esperanza gains enough strength by the end of the book to leave her house on Mango Street, she is reminded by one of the other characters that she must never forget who she is and where she came from: "You will always be Esperanza. You will always be Mango Street. You can't erase what you know. You can't forget who you are."

The House on Mango Street was a successful book. Many schools, from junior high schools through colleges, have used it in their classes. The book's success, however, didn't provide an easy life for Cisneros. After graduating from Iowa with a masters degree in creative writing, she worked as a part-time teacher. In 1986, she moved to Texas after receiving a fellowship (a financial award) to help her finish writing *My Wicked, Wicked Ways,* a book of poetry. After this volume was published in 1987, Cisneros's money ran out, and she could not find a job. She wanted to stay in Texas and even tried to start a private writing program. She passed out fliers in supermarkets to get interested people to join, but the program failed. Sad and broke, Cisneros had to leave Texas to take a teaching job at California State University in Chico, California.

Signs Major Publishing Contract

While in California, Cisneros received another grant of money to help her write a book of fiction. This new award from the National Endowment for the Arts revitalized Cisneros and inspired her to write *Women Hollering Creek and Other Stories.* Random House offered to publish the book in 1991, making Cisneros the first Chicana (Mexican American woman) to receive a major publishing contract for a work about Chicanas. The book, a series of short stories about strong Mexican American women living along the Texas-Mexico border, received praise from critics across the nation.

In 1994 another large publishing company issued *Loose Woman,* Cisneros's second collection of poetry. The main theme behind many of the poems in the book was love and its many powerful forms. A reviewer for *Publishers Weekly* wrote that the book again presents "a powerful, fiercely independent woman of Mexican heritage, though this time the innocence has long been lost."

Cisneros feels it is important for people of all races in America to understand the lives of Mexican Americans, especially Mexican American women. And Cisneros feels it is her duty to write about them. As she stated in *Authors and Artists for Young Adults,* "I feel very honored to give them a form in my writings and to be able to have this material to write about is a blessing."

For Further Information

Authors and Artists for Young Adults, Volume 9, Gale Research, 1992.
Glamour, November 1990, pp. 256-57.
Publishers Weekly, March 29, 1991, pp. 74-75; April 25, 1994, p. 61-62.
Washington Post Book World, June 9, 1991, p. 3.

Roberto Clemente

Professional baseball player
Born August 18, 1934, Carolina, Puerto Rico
Died December 31, 1972, near San Juan,
   Puerto Rico

"I like people that suffer because these peo-
ple have a different approach to life from the
people that have everything and don't know
what suffering is."

R oberto Clemente was a baseball star well loved by Puerto Ricans. As a right fielder for the Pittsburgh Pirates from 1955 to 1972, he won four National League batting titles, twelve Golden Glove awards, and was named the National League's Most Valuable Player in 1966. He was a proud man who demanded more respect for Hispanic players. His lifelong dream was to build a youth sports facility in Puerto Rico for poor children. In 1972, while flying relief supplies to earthquake victims in Nicaragua, his plane went down off the coast of Puerto Rico.

Clemente was born in 1934 in Puerto Rico, the youngest of the seven children of Melchor and Luisa Clemente. His father was a foreman on a sugarcane plantation, and his mother ran a grocery store for plantation workers. The young Clemente was raised to respect honesty, generosity, and his elders. "When I was a boy," he was quoted as saying in *Smithsonian,* "I realized what lovely persons my father and mother were. I learned the right way to live. I never heard any hate in my house. Not for anybody."

Another lesson Clemente learned from his parents was the value of working hard. When he was nine years old, he wanted to buy a bicycle. In order to earn money, he began delivering milk to his neighbors. He earned a penny a day. After three years, he had saved enough money for the bicycle. The experience of having to work hard for what he wanted stayed with Clemente all his life. "I am from the poor people," he said. "I represent the poor people. I like workers. I like people that suffer because these people have a different approach to life from the people that have everything and don't know what suffering is."

Signs First Baseball Contract

Clemente excelled at baseball as a child. He worked constantly and intensely at perfecting his skills. Even though his father told him he was too old to keep playing ball, he played amateur softball on the sandlots of his hometown of Carolina until he was 18 years old. At that time he was spotted by a scout from the professional hardball team in the Puerto Rican town of Santurce. He signed with the club for $40 per month, plus a $500 bonus.

Clemente was a star with the Santurce team for two seasons before he caught the attention of major league scouts. In 1954 the Los Angeles Dodgers signed him up and sent him to their minor league team in Montreal. At the time, a player who was not kept on a major league team's roster could be picked up by another team. When Clemente was not called up to the Dodgers by the end of the season, the Pittsburgh Pirates drafted him. He started the 1955 season as the Pirates' official right fielder.

Roberto Clemente

Clemente's career began without great fanfare as he slowly learned the routine in the big leagues. One major obstacle for him was the English language. "He found it difficult to make his feelings clear," said Joe L. Brown, who worked for the Pirates at the time. "He was an emotional person, a very sensitive person, and he was not understood."

Begins Compiling Superstar Stats

In 1960, however, Clemente began to make his presence known on the field. He hit .314 with 16 home runs and 94 runs batted in. He helped lead the Pirates to win both the National League pennant and the World Series.

Over the next 12 seasons, Clemente was a dominant force in professional baseball. He was famous for his incredible fielding skills, swift running, and powerful throwing. He thrilled fans by throwing out runners from remote spots in the outfield. Many times he threw strikes to home plate from more than 400 feet in the outfield. He was fearless in pursuit of the ball, diving into the grass and crashing into the wall.

Clemente's batting statistics were impressive as well. He trained to become a "spray hitter," scattering linedrive doubles and triples into the gaps between fielders. He was only the eleventh player in major league history to collect 3,000 hits in a career. His lifetime batting average was .317. For his heroics in the field and at the plate he was elected to the National League All Star team 12 times. After leading the Pirates to victory in the 1971 World Series, he was honored with the series's outstanding player award.

Misunderstood by Media

In spite of his achievements, Clemente had disappointments during his career. He suffered from numerous injuries and ailments, including back pain, stomach disorders, and tension headaches. Even after diligent study, he never completely mastered English. American sports writers had trouble understanding him, and his quotes in newspapers often contained grammar errors that he found embarrassing and insulting. Because of the language barrier, he believed he and other Hispanic players did not receive the recognition or respect they deserved.

Clemente always promoted Hispanic players and Hispanic pride. He took young

Hispanic players under his wing, helping them with their game. His large home in Puerto Rico, where he lived with his wife and three children, often was open to admiring fans. During the off-season he traveled around the island giving baseball clinics for children. "I go out to different towns, different neighborhoods," he said in *Smithsonian.* "I get kids together and talk about the importance of sports, the importance of being a good citizen, the importance of respecting their mother and father."

Dreams Cut Short

Clemente's dream was to build a sports complex to give Puerto Rican children opportunities to learn and to grow. At the end of the 1972 baseball season, he contemplated retiring from baseball to work full-time to develop his hometown sports camp for kids. Late that year, he was distracted from his decision by a massive earthquake that caused widespread disaster in Nicaragua. After organizing relief efforts from Puerto Rico, he went along to deliver the supplies in person. On December 31, 1972, Clemente died in the crash of a cargo plane that was carrying food to Nicaragua.

The world mourned the death of the great athlete and humanitarian. The Baseball Hall of Fame waived its five-year waiting period after a player's retirement and immediately elected Clemente to membership. His family continues to work on his Sports City in Carolina, Puerto Rico. The 304-acre complex provides children with baseball, basketball, swimming, and track training. Future plans include programs in drama, music, dance and folklore.

For Further Information

Gilbert, Thomas W., *Roberto Clemente,* Chelsea House, 1991.

O'Connor, Jim, *The Story of Roberto Clemente, All-Star Hero,* Dell, 1991.

Smithsonian, September 1993, pp. 136+.

Walker, Paul Robert, *Pride of Puerto Rico: The Life of Roberto Clemente,* Harcourt, Brace, Jovanovich, 1988.

Francisco Vásquez de Coronado

Spanish explorer
Born c. 1510, Salamanca, Spain
Died September 22, 1554, Mexico City, Mexico

"Coronado pushed the boundaries of New Spain far to the north, proving there were unimagined amounts of land to develop in America."

Francisco Vásquez de Coronado was a fearless Spanish explorer who continued Spain's relentless quest for gold into unmapped regions of the New World. He led the first European expeditions into the present-day southwestern United States. His men were the first Europeans to view the geographical wonders of the area, including the magnificent stone walls of the Grand Canyon.

Coronado was born around 1510, the second son of a noble Spanish family. Only the oldest son could inherit the family wealth, so Coronado chose to seek his fortune in the

Francisco Vásquez de Coronado

New World. In 1535 he arrived in Mexico (called New Spain by the Spanish) to work for Antonio de Mendoza, the first viceroy (the king's representative) of the region. Shortly afterward, Coronado married Beatriz de Estrada, a wealthy heiress. He successfully completed his first assignment—subduing a revolt by workers in the royal mines. For his deed, he was appointed governor of New Galicia, an area on the west coast of Mexico, in 1538.

The Spanish were still hoping to find gold in the vast, unknown territories to the north. No Europeans had ever ventured into these lands. Another explorer, Alvar Núñez Cabeza de Vaca (see **Alvar Núñez Cabeza de Vaca**), had reported hearing of seven great cities in a northern region called Cibola. A Franciscan friar named Fray Marcos de Niza was sent to verify reports of the supposed riches in this area. Upon his return, he claimed to have seen Cibola from a distance. Coronado and Mendoza were convinced they should send an expedition to find and conquer Cibola. Fray Marcos would be their guide.

Searches for Cities of Gold

In 1540 Coronado led a force of about 300 Spaniards and 1,000 Native Americans northward. They took along herds of cattle, sheep, goats, and swine for food. They marched slowly to Culiacán, the northernmost European settlement in New Spain. The slow pace frustrated Coronado. Once the group reached Culiacán, he chose 100 men as an advance army and led them ahead. He sent another smaller group to scout westward, and they traveled into present-day California.

Coronado led his group into present-day Colorado, then into present-day New Mexico. He came upon the town Fray Marcos identified as Cíbola and quickly captured it. Once there, however, Coronado realized it was no city of riches, only a poor village. He sent Fray Marcos back to Mexico in disgrace.

Amazing Geographical Discoveries

Thinking there might be other riches ahead, Coronado wanted to explore further. He also dreaded returning to Mexico as a failure. Coronado sent several small expeditions in different directions looking for gold. One group found ancient Hopi villages in present-day northern Arizona. Another arrived, amazed, at the edge of the Grand Canyon. The group tried to climb down its cliffs to the Colorado River. After three days, the Spaniards gave up and turned back.

A third party explored along the Rio Grande River and found an area the Pueblo called Tiguex, near present-day Albuquerque, New Mexico. Coronado joined them at Tiguex and settled down for the winter. Frictions soon developed between the Europeans and Native Americans: the Spanish demanded supplies and Pueblo women. The Pueblo revolted and Coronado spent the winter battling them. In one notorious incident, Coronado ordered two hundred Pueblo prisoners to be burned at the stake.

In the spring of 1541, Coronado set out once more in search of gold. A captured Pawnee guide, whom the Spanish had named "the Turk," had told the Spanish of a land of riches to the east, called "Quivira." Searching for Quivira, Coronado and his men crossed the Pecos River of New Mexico into the Texas panhandle, then moved north into the Great Plains. Local Native Americans often fled as the Spanish approached. They were fearful of the Spanish explorers' horses, animals that were new to the Americas. As the explorers moved through the plains, they were surprised to encounter large herds of animals they called "humpback oxen"—the American bison. Coronado sent his main force back to Tiguex with large supplies of meat from these animals.

Disappointment and a Long Trip Home

For five weeks, Coronado wandered westward in Texas. He then turned north to explore present-day Oklahoma and Kansas, crossing the Canadian and Arkansas Rivers along the way. When he finally arrived at Quivira, he found neither gold nor silver—only poor Native American camps. Coronado was crushed by disappointment at not finding a city of treasures. He left three missionaries to convert the native people of Quivira to Christianity. He then turned back toward Tiguex. After reaching the area, he was seriously injured in a riding accident. Coronado stayed at Tiguex to recover and to wait out the winter.

Coronado's difficult journey home to Mexico took about six months. Discouraged Spanish soldiers deserted at every opportunity. When Coronado arrived in Mexico City in June 1542, he was accompanied by fewer than one hundred men. Viceroy Mendoza was angered by what he considered a wasted expedition, but allowed Coronado to continue as governor of New Galicia for a few more years. In 1545 the explorer was tried for cruelty toward Native Americans during his travels. Although cleared of all charges, Coronado lost his governorship. He retired to Mexico City where he died in 1554.

Coronado and his men considered their expedition a failure. However, the journals they kept, along with the reports they sent back to Mexico and Spain, were of great value in the future. Coronado pushed the boundaries of New Spain far to the north, proving there were unimagined amounts of land to develop in America. The maps he made would aid other explorers in their quest to go farther.

For Further Information

Hispanic, October 1990, p. 38.

Jensen, Malcolm C., *Francisco Coronado,* Watts, 1974.

Syme, Ronald, *Francisco Coronado and the Seven Cities of Gold,* Morrow, 1965.

Udall, Stewart L., *To the Inland Empire: Coronado and Our Spanish Legacy,* Doubleday, 1987.

Zadra, Dan, *Coronado: Explorer of the Southwest (1510-1554),* Creative Education, 1988.

Placido Domingo

Opera singer
Born January 21, 1941, Madrid, Spain

"Living in Mexico made me feel very much Latin American wherever I went to perform. Whenever I traveled to Puerto Rico, Argentina, Chile, or any Latin country, I felt very much at home."

In Spanish, Placido Domingo's name means "peaceful Sunday." In fact, Domingo's schedule is anything but peaceful. As the busiest and one of the most well known opera tenors in the world, he sings in 80 performances per year and has made more than 150 recordings. He also conducts orchestras and helps organize new opera companies around the world.

Domingo has also starred in films and television productions. He has even recorded popular music with singers like John Denver. He still tries to find time for more casual events, like singing the national anthem at a Los Angeles Dodgers baseball game. Because he travels constantly for performances, he has homes in London, Los Angeles, New York, Vienna, and Monaco. One of his favorite possessions is a needlepoint pillow that reads, "If I rest, I rust."

Domingo was born in 1941 into a musical family in Madrid, Spain. His parents, Placido Domingo and Pepita Embil, were professional singers who specialized in *zarzuelas,* Spanish folk operettas (romantic comedies featuring singing and dancing). When Domingo was six years old, his parents moved the

Placido Domingo

family to Mexico City, Mexico, where they organized an operetta company.

Even though his parents made him a Mexican citizen while he was still young, Domingo never forgot his Spanish roots. When he was older, he reapplied for his Spanish citizenship. The years he eventually spent in Mexico, however, had a great effect on him. He learned about and came to embrace other Hispanic cultures. "Living in Mexico made me feel very much Latin American wherever I went to perform," he related to

Rosie Carbo in *Hispanic.* "Whenever I traveled to Puerto Rico, Argentina, Chile, or any Latin country, I felt very much at home."

Musical Training Starts Early

Domingo's musical training began with piano lessons at the age of eight. By the age of nine he had won a song-and-dance contest and begun singing children's roles in his parents' operettas. During his high school years at the Instituto Mexico, he played soccer (a great fan of the sport to this day, he tries to schedule a month off during World Cup competition). He even tried the dangerous sport of bullfighting, performing as an amateur matador at private fiestas.

Domingo then studied at the National Conservatory of Music in Mexico City. He made his first stage appearance at age 19 with the Mexico City National Opera in *Rigoletto,* by Italian composer Giuseppe Verdi. He started out as a baritone singer, but switched to tenor on the advice of his teachers. He had to force his voice at first to reach certain high notes, but he soon mastered the technique. Singing is a balancing act: a singer must find a blend between vocal sounds, emotions, and intellect. One of the reasons Domingo is so highly esteemed as a musician is because he masterfully achieves this balance of technique and emotional understanding of his art.

In 1961 Domingo met and married Marta Ornelas, a Mexican opera star. The following year the couple joined the Israel National Opera Company in Tel Aviv and spent two years there (Domingo is fluent in several languages, including Hebrew). In 1965 the couple had a son and Marta Ornelas retired from the stage. Domingo then came to the United States to audition for the New York City Opera. His performances the first season went unnoticed by New York's music critics. The very next year, however, he caught the attention of those same critics for his singing and acting in the ultramodern opera *Don Rodrigo,* by Argentine composer Alberto Ginastera.

Takes Risks for His Art

Domingo is a risk-taker. At the age of 27 (still young by opera standards) he attempted to sing a very difficult role in the opera *Loengrin,* by German composer Richard Wagner. The part requires the tenor to sing a tricky combination of musical notes that strain—and can even damage—vocal chords. Domingo succeeded, but it took months for him to recover his voice and confidence.

In 1968 he made his official debut with the prestigious Metropolitan Opera in New York and received excellent reviews. Because Domingo undertook such a breakneck schedule, many predicted that he would burn out. Fortunately, he didn't have to use his voice to practice. Able to memorize his parts, he studied the music at a piano. He knew 90 operas—30 of them well enough to perform at a moment's notice.

For two days before a performance, he and his wife Marta were in the habit of escaping to a quiet resort in northern New York. There the singer rested, read sports magazines, walked, and swam. To protect his voice on the day of a performance, he did not talk at all. Since Domingo is outgoing, energetic, and friendly, this is the most difficult of sacrifices.

Talent Carries Over to Acting and Conducting

In 1984 Domingo made his debut as a conductor. He led New York's Metropolitan Opera in a performance of *La Boheme,* by Italian composer Giacomo Puccini. He soon expanded his talents by turning his operatic stage performances into related roles in films. In 1986 he starred in director Franco Zeffirelli's film adaptation of Verdi's opera *Othello.* His performance won rave reviews. He has also starred in Zeffirelli's version of Verdi's *La Traviata* and director Francesco

Rossi's film of the opera *Carmen,* by French composer Georges Bizet.

Domingo amazes the music world with his boundless energy and enthusiasm. He is optimistic about his future and avoids talk of retirement. In 1993 he celebrated his twenty-fifth anniversary at the Metropolitan Opera by singing at a gala opening night before a crowd of thrilled fans. The following year he reprised his collaboration with fellow tenors José Carreras and Luciano Pavarotti, participating in a landmark concert that resulted in a critically acclaimed and best-selling recording. He continues to sing and to conduct. He hopes to someday establish an opera training school in Monte Carlo.

Domingo has received many honors over the years, including two Emmy awards and six Grammy awards. One award of which he is most proud is the Order of the Aztec Eagle—Mexico's highest honor. He was given the presitigious award by the Mexican government in 1985 for helping to save victims from the rubble left by a devastating earthquake that shook Mexico City. He spent the following year performing nothing but benefit concerts for the many victims who had been left homeless.

For Further Information

Hispanic, August 1992, pp. 47-49.

Stefoff, Rebecca, *Placido Domingo,* Chelsea House, 1992.

Time, September 27, 1993, pp. 82-83.

Sheila E.

Singer, songwriter, musician
Born c. 1958, Oakland, California

"I've always wanted to incorporate a lot of the Latin into the albums, but I didn't know how. I thought that if I put in too much Latin, people wouldn't like it. I think that it was a mistake to think that people wouldn't accept me as I was."

Sheila E. first achieved fame in the early 1980s as a duet partner with pop superstar Prince. The drummer and singer then found success on her own with her first solo album, *The Glamorous Life.* The 1984 record was a hit. Her 1985 follow-up album, *Romance 1600,* proved Sheila E. was a musician with a wide range. Pamela Bloom pointed out in *High Fidelity* that "Sheila demonstrates on *Romance 1600* how equally at home she is in fusion, funk, pop, and salsa, as well as in the traditional r & b dance mix."

Sheila E. was born Sheila Escovedo sometime in the late 1950s in Oakland, California, to Pete and Juanita Escovedo. Her father was famous for his drum work with the rock group Santana and, later, the Latin band Azteca. Her brothers also became drummers. When Sheila E. was three, she began to watch her father practice his conga drums. She'd sit in front of him and copy him, mirroring his style. Because of this "mirroring," she developed a lefthanded style on the drums, which allows her to beat them faster and harder than most drummers.

Sheila E.

Her father had hoped she would become a symphony performer and sent her to violin lessons when she was ten. She quit after five years and switched to more popular instruments such as guitar and keyboard. As a teenager she believed she had a greater chance of becoming an Olympic athlete than a successful musician. She spent much of her time playing football with neighborhood boys and challenging her friends to footraces.

Joins Father's Band

Despite her attraction to sports, Sheila E. kept practicing the drums. While still a teenager, she was offered professional music jobs. Her father, who thought she was still too young to become a professional drummer, eventually let her fill in for an ailing percussionist in his band. In her first appearance with the group, she performed a solo that received an overwhelming response from the audience. "When I heard that ovation," she related to Bloom, "I had this feeling I had never had in my whole life.... It felt like the ultimate." Soon after, she quit high school to concentrate on her musical career.

Sheila E. toured Europe and Asia with her father's band and recorded two albums as part of that group. She also worked as a studio musician for stars such as Lionel Richie, Diana Ross, and Herbie Hancock. In 1978 she met Prince (as he was then called). "When I first saw him, I just thought he was this cute guy standing against the wall," she told Bloom. "But when we met, he was impressed, too, because he had heard of *me.*"

Although the two often worked together writing songs, Sheila E. did not record with Prince until 1984, when she sang a duet with him on his hit single "Erotic City." He showed her how to compose songs faster than she had been, helped her create a sexy new image, and advised her to go solo. He even helped produce *The Glamorous Life.* He also gave her more experience and publicity by hiring her as the opening act for his "Purple Rain" tour. She was nervous at first, but soon learned to enjoy her new role in the spotlight.

Returns to Her Roots

Sheila E.'s next albums were not tremendous hits, but they established her as a songwriter and performer of note. *Romance 1600,* included "Love Bizarre," another duet with Prince that reached near the top of the charts. On her third album, released in 1987 and simply titled *Sheila E.,* she involved her family. Her father, mother, brothers, and sister sang or played backup on many of the songs.

On her 1991 effort, *Sex Cymbal,* Sheila E. returned to her Latin musical roots. "I've always wanted to incorporate a lot of the Latin into the albums, but I didn't know how," she explained to Karen Schoemer in *Interview.* "I thought that if I put in too much Latin, people wouldn't like it. I think that it was a mistake to think that people wouldn't accept me as I was." In 1993 Sheila E. lent her world-renowned percussion talents to another Latin recording, Gloria Estefan's (see **Gloria Estefan**) *Mi Tierra.*

For Further Information

High Fidelity, January 1986, pp. 64-65+.
Hispanic, July 1991, p. 54.
Interview, March 1991, p. 24.
People, May 6, 1991, pp. 29-30.

Jaime Escalante

Educator
Born December 31, 1930, La Paz, Bolivia

"It's the only thing I can do."

In 1982 18 students from the mostly Hispanic Garfield High School in East Los Angeles passed the Advanced Placement (AP) calculus exam. This math test enabled them to receive college credit for classes they had taken in high school. It is a very difficult test, and only a small percentage of students in the United States even attempt it. The students' achievement was remarkable because Garfield High was previously known mostly for its gangs, drug use, and low academic standards.

The driving force behind the students' success was Jaime Escalante, a teacher who challenged them to reach their full potential. The achievements of Escalante and his students caught the attention of the nation in 1988 when a popular movie, *Stand and Deliver,* retold their stories. Afterward, U.S. President Ronald Reagan called Escalante a hero on national television.

Escalante was born in 1930 in La Paz, Bolivia. After receiving his education in that country, he became a highly respected mathematics and science teacher in high schools in La Paz. Political unrest in Bolivia, however, forced Escalante, his wife Fabiola, and their son Jaime, Jr., to flee the country in 1964 and settle in California. Escalante wanted to resume his teaching career, but he spoke no English and his teaching license was of no value in the United States. While working as a busboy and later as a cook, Escalante taught himself English. He then became a computer parts tester.

Although Escalante did well at his new job, he missed teaching. For seven years he attended night classes at California State University. In 1974, after receiving a bachelor's degree in mathematics and a teaching

Jaime Escalante

atrics. To illustrate a point about percentages, he donned an apron and a chef's hat, set an apple on his desk, then chopped it in half with a large butcher's knife. He encouraged his students to scrape the graffiti off their desks. He then invited them to help paint the classroom, decorating it with Los Angeles Lakers posters afterward. In his lessons, Escalante used sports language and business techniques. He often challenged students to handball contests on Saturdays, telling them that if they won, they would receive an automatic "A." If he won, they had to do their homework. The students were shocked to find that the middle-aged Escalante won every time—he had been a handball star in Bolivia.

Escalante also got his students' attention by embarrassing them. If a student was tardy to class, he or she was made to sit in a kindergarten-sized chair. If a student's attention wandered in class, he or she was pelted with a little red pillow. Escalante was also quick to give encouragement if his students performed well in class. He fought for money to provide decent breakfasts and summer scholarships for them. He won their respect because he was strict but fair and kept a sense of humor in the classroom. His students began to increase their math skills.

license, he was hired as a teacher at Garfield High School.

Introduces New Math Methods

On his first day at the school, Escalante realized the students were in trouble. Many of them had to count on their fingers when figuring out math problems on the chalkboard. Almost all the students came to class unprepared and without supplies. The toughness of many of the teenagers at Garfield frightened Escalante. Fights between rival gang members were common, and nonstudents wandered the halls causing trouble. The adult staff was intimidated and discouraged.

To gain the students' interest, Escalante began skipping lectures and resorting to the-

Hard Work and Determination Win Out

In 1979 Escalante held his first calculus class. Even though only five students attended, four of them went on to pass the difficult AP calculus test. The next two years were even more successful for the teacher and his students. In 1982, however, Escalante suffered a minor heart attack. That same year 14 of his 18 calculus students were accused of cheating on the AP test. Because their errors appeared suspiciously similar, they had to take a new, more difficult test. Escalante was angry, but his students were determined to prove they had mastered the work. Two students decided not to attend college, but the other 12 returned to take the new test. All 12 passed.

The incident received much local publicity and caught the attention of film producers. Many believed that the students' scores would never have been questioned if they had not been Hispanic and from the poor Garfield High School. Filmmakers approached Escalante about making a movie of his triumphs and he gave them the go-ahead. He allowed Edward James Olmos (see **Edward James Olmos**), the actor who was to play him in the movie, to spend 18 hours a day with him for a month.

The success of the 1988 movie *Stand and Deliver* made Garfield and Escalante symbols of educational and personal achievement in the face of great odds. It helped attract the attention of businesses, which donated $750,000 to the school to help update its teaching materials and equipment.

Students Continue Academic Success

In the spring of 1988 Escalante watched as seven of the twelve students from his 1982 class graduated from the engineering program at the University of Southern California. Over the years, more of his students have gone on to graduate from University of California campuses and Ivy League schools. Their fields of study have been diverse, ranging from engineering to teaching to law. For his

work with these students, Escalante has received many awards, including the 1989 White House Hispanic Heritage Award and the 1990 American Institute for Public Service Jefferson Award.

In September 1991 Escalante began teaching math at Hiram High School in Sacramento, California. He continued to offer support to the Saturday-and-summer training program he started for students and teachers at East Los Angeles College in 1983. In 1991 he also developed an award-winning public television series on math, science, and careers called *Futures.* A video selection from that series, "Math ... Who Needs It?," was the Blue Ribbon winner at the 1992 American Film and Video Festival. When asked by *People*'s Charles E. Cohen why he continues teaching after he has faced so many obstacles, Escalante replied, "It's the only thing I can do."

For Further Information

Booklist, January 1, 1993, p. 818.

Mathews, Jay, *Escalante: The Best Teacher in America,* Henry Holt, 1988.

Newsweek, July 20, 1992, pp. 58-59.

People, September 16, 1991, pp. 111-12.

Gloria Estefan

Pop singer, songwriter
Born 1958, Havana, Cuba

"You can't sit there and wallow. You weep for what's gone and then you move ahead."

From her Hispanic roots to the pop music mainstream, Gloria Estefan is an example of the American dream come true. She started her musical career with the Miami Sound Machine, originally a Cuban American quartet that performed popular music with a Latin influence. The band grew from being a sensation in Spanish-speaking countries to international popularity due to the talent and hard work of Estefan and her husband, Emilio.

Estefan was born Gloria Fajardo in 1958 in Havana, Cuba. Her mother was a schoolteacher. Her father, José Manuel Fajardo, was a bodyguard to President Fulgencio Batista at the time of Estefan's birth. The following year Fidel Castro and others overthrew Batista and installed a Communist government in Cuba. The Fajardo family quickly fled to the United States. José Manuel Fajardo was then recruited by the Central Intelligence Agency into a band of anti-Castro Cubans sent to invade Cuba. The invasion took place on April 17, 1961, at the Bay of Pigs. It failed, and Fajardo was taken prisoner. After President John F. Kennedy won the release of the prisoners, Fajardo returned to the United States, joined the U.S. Army, and served two years in the Vietnam War.

As a child, Estefan took classical guitar lessons, but found them tedious. She preferred to write poetry. She had no idea that she would some day become a popular music star, but music played a very important role for her as a teenager. When her father returned from the war, he became ill with the disabling disease of multiple sclerosis, possibly as a result from being exposed to the herbicide Agent Orange while in Vietnam. Estefan's mother worked to support the family during the day while attending school at night. The young Estefan was left to care for her father and younger sister. With little in the way of a social life, she turned to music for distraction.

"When my father was ill, music was my escape," Estefan told Richard Harrington of the *Washington Post*. "I would lock myself up in my room for hours and just sing. I wouldn't cry—I refused to cry…. Music was the only way I had to just let go, so I sang for fun and for emotional catharsis."

Joins Future Husband's Band

In 1975 Estefan met keyboardist Emilio Estefan, leader of a band called the Miami Latin Boys. When he heard her voice, he asked her to perform as lead singer with his band. At first, she sang only on weekends because she was attending the University of Miami. A year and a half after she joined the group (by then renamed the Miami Sound Machine), they recorded their first album. *Renacer* was a collection of disco pop and original ballads sung in Spanish.

Although Estefan was somewhat plump and very shy when she joined the band, she slimmed down with a rigorous exercise program and worked to overcome her stagefright. Gradually, her professional relationship with Emilio Estefan turned personal, and in 1978 they married. Their son Nayib was born two years later.

Between 1981 and 1983 the Miami Sound Machine recorded four Spanish-language albums made up of ballads, disco, pop, and sambas (the music for a Brazilian dance with African origins). The group had dozens of hit songs in Spanish-speaking countries such as Venezuela, Peru, Panama, and Honduras, but were unknown in the United States.

Fame in the U.S.A.

The group's first North American hit was the disco single "Dr. Beat" from *Eyes of Innocence,* their first album to contain songs sung in English. "Conga," a rousing dance number from the album, became the first single to crack *Billboard* magazine's pop, dance, black, and Latin charts at the same time. Estefan and the group, whose members had changed over the years, prided themselves on the combination of Latin rhythms, rhythm and blues, and mainstream pop that made their music special.

In 1986 the album *Primitive Love,* the band's first recording entirely in English, set off a string of hit singles. "Bad Boys" and "Words Get in the Way" jumped onto *Billboard*'s Top 10 pop chart. Extensive tours and music videos on MTV and VH1 made the Miami Sound Machine a leading American band. Their next album, *Let It Loose,* released in 1987, had several hit singles: "Betcha Say That," "1-2-3," and the ballad "Anything for You." Estefan gradually became the star attraction, and the group came to be known as Gloria Estefan and the Miami Sound Machine, or sometimes simply Gloria Estefan. Some people said Estefan

Gloria Estefan

reminded them of a less-controversial, Hispanic version of Madonna.

Despite the group's popularity with English-speaking listeners, the Estefans have not forgotten their roots. They are always working on Spanish-language projects. The title of their 1989 album, *Cuts Both Ways,* refers to their intention to appeal to both English- and Spanish-speaking audiences. For this album, in addition to singing, Estefan was involved in the planning, producing, composing of music, and writing of lyrics. In 1993 she released *Mi Tierra,* an all-Spanish album of original melodies that recall classic Afro-Cuban songs.

Suffers Back Injury

After the couple's son Nayib was born, Emilio Estefan gave up his position as keyboardist with the band. He devoted his energy to publicity, business arrangements, and spending time with his son. A close family, the Estefans arranged to meet as often as possible during tours. In March 1990, while Emilio Estefan and Nayib were traveling with the group, the band's bus was involved in an accident on a snowy highway in Pennsylvania. Nayib suffered a fractured shoulder and Emilio Estefan received minor head and hand injuries. Gloria Estefan suffered a critically broken back.

In a four-hour operation several days later, surgeons repaired Estefan's spine by inserting two eight-inch steel rods for support. Doctors feared she might never walk again, and the Estefans retired to their home on Biscayne Bay in Florida to recuperate. Thanks to extensive physical therapy, intense determination, and the support of her family and fans, Estefan made what many consider a miraculous comeback. "You can't sit there and wallow," she told *People*'s Pam Lambert. "You weep for what's gone and then you move ahead." Estefan returned to the stage with an appearance on television's American Music Awards in January 1991, and launched a yearlong tour to celebrate her comeback album, *Into the Light*.

In 1992 Florida was battered by Hurricane Andrew. Knowing the pain of coming back from injury, the Estefans jumped into the relief effort with energy. They quickly established relief centers in their South Miami studio-office complex. Estefan then released an inspirational ballad, "Always Tomorrow," and donated all proceeds to the hurricane relief. Afterward, the Estefans recruited celebrity friends to join them in a star-studded benefit concert at Miami's Joe Robbie Stadium. The effort raised two million dollars for victims of the disastrous hurricane.

For Further Information

Gonzalez, Fernando, *Gloria Estefan, Cuban-American Singing Star,* Millbrook Press, 1993.
Hispanic, September 1993, pp. 102-03.
People, October 12, 1992, p. 47.
Stefoff, Rebecca, *Gloria Estefan,* Chelsea House, 1991.
Washington Post, July 17, 1988.

Emilio Estevez

Actor, screenwriter, director
Born May 12, 1962, New York, New York

"My dad taught me to trust myself and to always search for the truth in whatever I was doing."

In the mid-1980s, a group of young actors came to be known as Hollywood's "Brat Pack." The talented and sucessful—and sometimes brash—group was unofficially led by Emilio Estevez. Estevez, who is also a screenwriter and director, grew up in a family loaded with talent. His father, Martin Sheen, and brother, Charlie Sheen (see **Charlie Sheen**), are well-established actors. Mother Janet is a film producer, and siblings Ramon and Renee Estevez are breaking into the business.

Estevez was born in 1962 in New York City, but moved with his family to Malibu, California, six years later. His father, who had been born Ramón Estevez, changed his

Spanish name to avoid being typecast in films. Young Estevez, with his sandy hair and blue eyes, kept the original family name because he could easily play mainstream roles. Also, he wanted to earn his own reputation rather than enter the industry on his father's famous name.

Estevez began performing at an early age in school plays and in 8mm films he made with his brother Charlie and neighborhood friends Chris and Sean Penn. He also began writing at an early age. One effort was a science fiction story he wrote as a second grader and tried to sell to the producers of television's *Night Gallery* series. The story was rejected, but Estevez wasn't discouraged. He kept writing, and in high school he starred in a play he wrote about Vietnam War veterans. It was titled *Echoes of an Era* and was directed by his friend Sean Penn. Most of Estevez's attention in high school, however, was focused on sports, especially soccer and track.

Emilio Estevez

First Movie Roles

Knowing he could not compete professionally in sports, Estevez soon returned to acting. "I knew I had an ability to perform from an early age, to really excel at it," he wrote in an early studio biography, as quoted by *Hispanic*'s Elena Kellner. "So I began taking acting lessons seriously and started auditioning." He landed his first professional acting job right after his graduation from Santa Monica High School. It was a role in an after-school TV special, *Seventeen Going on Nowhere.* He made his motion picture debut in 1982, playing opposite Matt Dillon in *Tex,* a film based on a novel by best-selling author S. E. Hinton.

In 1983 Estevez appeared in another screen adaptation of a Hinton novel, *The Outsiders,* a story about a teen gang. The movie featured many other up-and-coming actors, including Dillon, Tom Cruise, Rob Lowe, Diane Lane, Ralph Macchio, and Patrick Swayze. Estevez achieved recognition the following year in *Repo Man,* in which he portrayed a punk rocker who takes a job as an automobile repossessor. To prepare for the role Estevez immersed himself in punk rock music and visited punk clubs.

Estevez finally caught the attention of critics in 1985 when he played a very different role, that of a high school jock in *The*

Breakfast Club. Directed by John Hughes, the hit film follows five students from different cliques in a suburban Chicago high school who have to spend a Saturday together in detention. At first, the characters want nothing to do with each other and tempers flare. As the day progresses, however, they begin to open up to each other, discussing their families and their dreams. By day's end, having learned to look beyond their teen stereotypes, they reach out to each other and become friends.

Late in 1985, Estevez appeared in *That Was Then…This Is Now,* a film for which he also wrote the screenplay. The movie is based on another novel by S. E. Hinton, which Estevez had read while filming *Tex.* The author herself suggested that Estevez play the starring role in the story about two teenage boys whose long-time friendship is threatened when one of them falls in love. "I came across a project that I became passionate about," he told *Teen* magazine. "I wanted to bring it to the screen because it's a film about young people that's honest."

Makes Hollywood History

Estevez went on to increase his involvement in film by starring in *Wisdom* with Demi Moore. It tells the story of a young man who travels across the country entering banks and vandalizing mortgage files to stop the banks from foreclosing on farmers' mortgages. Although panned by most critics, the 1987 film made Estevez—at age 23—the youngest person ever to have written, directed, and starred in a major motion picture.

Estevez continued his writing/directing/starring role in the 1990 comedy *Men at Work.* The film, about California garbage-men who become involved with a murder and an ocean-polluting chemical company, also starred Charlie Sheen. Again, critics were unkind in their view of Estevez's work. Ralph Novak, writing in *People,* believed that "finding things to like in this film resembles—what else?—garbage picking. You have to poke through the junk to get to the good stuff."

Estevez's work in two films that both spawned sequels, however, was immensely popular. In 1988 he starred in *Young Guns.*

The hit film, which follows the exploits of Billy the Kid (Estevez) and his gang, also featured Kiefer Sutherland and Lou Diamond Phillips. All three actors, along with others, reprised their roles in the 1990 sequel, *Young Guns 2.*

In 1987 Estevez had starred with Richard Dreyfuss and Madeleine Stowe in the comedy/thriller Stakeout. The film, about a pair of police detectives who stake out a woman's apartment hoping to find her boyfriend, who had broken out of prison, was a success. Six years later, Estevez and Dreyfuss teamed up again in *Stakeout 2.* This time they had to keep an eye on a woman who was going to testify against the Mob.

Faces Pressures of Hollywood

In 1992 Estevez married Paula Abdul, the equally famous dancer/singer. With the media and their fans following their every move, the couple found it hard to lead a private life. The pressures of a Hollywood marriage soon proved to be too great. The couple separated in the spring of 1994.

Estevez tries to keep his fame in perspective. To help him remain grounded, he remembers lessons his father has taught him.

Although he realizes his job is no more important than any other, he tries to remain focused on his work. "My dad taught me to trust myself," he said, as quoted by Kellner, "and to always search for the truth in whatever I was doing."

For Further Information

Hispanic, May 1994, pp. 14-18.
People, September 17, 1990, pp. 13-14.
Teen, September 1982; March 1985; July 1985; February 1991, pp. 34-35.

José Feliciano

Singer, guitarist
Born September 10, 1945, Lares, Puerto Rico

"I have tried to change the image of blind performers. I don't wear glasses, just like deaf people don't wear earmuffs."

José Monserrate Feliciano is a musician who overcame the obstacles of blindness and poverty to excel as a popular performer. He first became a hit with Spanish-speaking audiences in the United States and Latin America in the early 1960s. He then exploded on the English-language pop scene in 1968 with his stylized version of "Light My Fire," a song originally recorded by the rock group the Doors. He gained further notice that year when he gave a controversial performance of the "Star Spangled Banner" at a Detroit Tigers baseball game.

Feliciano has blended rock, soul, jazz, blues, classical, and Latin sounds into his own highly personal style. This, combined with his masterful guitar playing, has won him praise. He is the only performer to have won Grammy awards in two language categories. Throughout his career, he has downplayed his blindness, never letting the handicap slow him down or overshadow his talent. "I have tried to change the image of blind performers," he told a reporter for the *Grand Rapids Press.* "I don't wear glasses, just like deaf people don't wear earmuffs."

Feliciano was born in Lares, Puerto Rico, in 1945. He was the second of 12 children born to a very poor family. His father was a farmer and a longshoreman (someone who loads and unloads ships at a seaport). To find a better life, the family moved to a Latino section of New York City in 1950. Feliciano was born with glaucoma, an eye disease that made him blind. Because of his blindness, he was unable to participate in sports and other activities. At an early age he turned to music. He began beating out rhythms on a tin cracker can when he was three years old. At six he taught himself to play the concertina (a type of accordion) by listening to records for hours each day. He went on to master other instruments, including the banjo, mandolin, harmonica, organ, piano, and drums.

Combines Influences for a Unique Style

At first, Feliciano's chief musical influence was the Latin American sound his father urged him to imitate. Soon he was drawn to soul music, then rock and roll. He later became familiar with classical music, thanks to school teachers who recognized his talent. As a result, Feliciano developed a truly unique style. A reporter for *Time* once

José Feliciano

Central and South America. His popularity in the United States came slowly. In 1968, however, he scored his first big English-language hit with his soulful remake of "Light My Fire." *Feliciano,* the album on which the song appeared, rocketed to the top of the charts, and he was in demand for TV programs, concerts, and personal appearances.

Feliciano's success was sometimes coupled with conflict. During a series of concerts in England, the blind performer had a problem. English law forbade the entry of his seeing-eye dog into the country. It was a problem for the musician not only because he needed the dog for navigation, but also because she had become his onstage trademark. The helpful canine led the singer to his stool in the center of the stage at the beginning of each performance and returned to bow with him at the end. Because of this law, Feliciano did not return to England for several years.

Star-Spangled Controversy

One of Feliciano's most memorable performances was his unusual, stylized version of the "Star Spangled Banner," sung before a 1968 World Series baseball game at Detroit's Tiger Stadium. His blues-rock version of the national anthem was the first truly nontraditional interpretation of the song performed before a national audience. The stadium switchboard was flooded with calls. Some listeners were outraged and found Feliciano's "Spanish soul" treatment of the anthem unpatriotic. Others thought he gave the song a refreshing new twist. His follow-up recording of the "Star Spangled Banner" sold very well. At that year's Grammy awards ceremonies, he was named best male pop singer and best new artist.

described it as a cross between "[pop singer] Johnny Mathis and [soul singer] Ray Charles with a Latin American flavor and a classical-tinged guitar backing."

Feliciano made his first public performance at the age of nine at El Teatro Puerto Rico in Spanish Harlem (an area of New York City). Soon he was playing at local events, talent shows, and public assemblies. By the age of 16 he was contributing to the family income by playing pop, flamenco (a Spanish gypsy dance), and folk music in coffee houses. The next year, when his father lost his job, Feliciano dropped out of school to perform full-time to help support his family. He quickly became a hit with audiences throughout the East and Midwest.

At 17 Feliciano signed a recording contract with RCA Records. Because most of his recordings over the next few years were in Spanish, he became a pop sensation in

Feliciano continued to enjoy stardom as a recording artist, performer, and composer over the next decade. He wrote the music for several films and television shows, including the theme to *Chico and the Man.* His Christmas song, "Feliz Navidad," released in 1970, is now a holiday standard. Even though he released only a handful of albums during the 1970s, he remained a frequent television guest and a major concert draw.

Returns to Latin Roots

During the 1980s Feliciano returned to recording Spanish-language albums. The recordings garnered much praise and his international reputation grew. He received Grammy awards for best Latin pop performance in 1983, 1986, 1989, and 1990. In 1991, at the first annual Latin Music Expo, he was presented with the event's first-ever Lifetime Achievement Award.

In 1991 Feliciano branched out to take a job as a Saturday morning disc jockey for a radio station in Connecticut, not far from his home. Besides playing a mixture of old and new songs, he chats with callers, tells "insider" stories about the music world, and occasionally plays his guitar or sings a song. He makes time for 20 to 30 benefit concerts per year for charity organizations that help the blind. He and his wife, Susan, have two children. To spend more time with his family, Feliciano has given up extended concert tours.

For Further Information

Contemporary Musicians, Volume 10, Gale, 1994.
Detroit News, September 6, 1991, p. B1.
Grand Rapids Press, December 20, 1991, p. B6.
Time, September 27, 1968, p. 78.

Joseph A. Fernandez

Educational administrator, former New York City Public Schools chancellor
Born December 13, 1935, East Harlem, New York

"I'm leaving here with my head held high and I can sleep well at night knowing that I did the best thing for the children of New York."

J oseph A. Fernandez has devoted his entire professional life to improving educational opportunities for American students. In 1990 he became chancellor (superintendent) of New York City's public school district. With almost one million children, the district is the largest in the United States. At the time Fernandez took over, the city's school system was hurting financially, and its large administration was too slow to respond to the needs of students. Fernandez quickly made changes that pushed the district in a new direction. But the style that won him the job in the first place—high energy, single-mindedness, and a desire to experiment—also cost him his job after just three years.

Fernandez was born in 1935 in East Harlem, New York, to Angela and Joseph Fernandez, Sr., both of whom were of Puerto Rican heritage. His mother worked as a seamstress, then as a maid at Columbia University in New York. His father took whatever work he could find: washing windows, making deliveries, and driving a cab and a bus.

In his youth, Fernandez did not have a great respect for education. He attended parochial schools (private schools run by churches or other religious organizations) until the tenth grade, then ended up being expelled for skipping classes. He then entered a public high school but dropped out before graduating. Most of the time he hung out on the streets of his neighborhood with a local gang, the Riffs. And he did drugs—almost overdosing twice on heroin.

Gains Education in the Military

Fernandez finally began to turn his life around after joining the U.S. Air Force in the early 1950s. As he wrote in his autobiography, *Tales Out of School,* "I was not yet out of the woods with drugs, but I was on my way to being an educated man." While he was in the service, he spent time in Japan and Korea and completed courses to earn his high school diploma. Fernandez returned home in 1956, married his high school sweetheart, Lily Pons, and entered Columbia University with money from the military. He eventually completed his bachelor's degree at the University of Miami in 1963. Immediately afterward he began teaching mathematics at Coral Park High School in Miami, part of the Dade County school system.

"The fourth largest in the nation, the Dade County school system was an ideal training ground for Fernandez," wrote Thomas Toch in *U.S. News & World Report.* Fernandez moved up the academic ladder quickly. After only a year, he became chairperson of the math department. Over the next 20 years, he held a wide variety of positions—principal, contract negotiator, assistant superintendent, and superintendent of the Dade County system.

As superintendent of Dade County public schools from 1987 to 1989, Fernandez showed the creative skills that would later win him the job in New York City. He started Saturday computer and music classes; he persuaded Miami businesses to contribute money and space for school activities; he convinced Miami voters to pass a $980 million school bond issue; and most of all, as Tony Hiss noted in the *New Yorker,* Fernandez constantly found "new ways to teach both inner-city and suburban kids and [gave] them, along with knowledge, self-regard and pride in being citizens."

Sees Chancellorship as a Challenge

Fernandez took the job in New York City in 1990 because it was the toughest and most challenging in the field of American education. For years the district had been poorly managed. At that time, only about half of the $6,100 New York City spent on each high school student actually went to the schools. Fernandez went to work immediately to cut the waste. "In two weeks," Toch noted, "he cut his 5,200-person central staff by 400, suspended two principals, and ordered a local superintendent fired." He also appointed panels to study everything from classroom curricula (the lessons taught) to classroom overcrowding.

In his first year, Fernandez introduced two major reform measures. The first ended the building tenure system. Under this old system, elementary and junior high school principals could not be fired from their positions if they had served in that capacity at the same school for five or more years—even if they neglected their duties to the students and teachers. Fernandez abolished the system and fired many negligent principals.

The second measure was his School-Based Management/Shared Decision-Making (SBM) program. The program, which he had developed in Miami, decreased the number of high-level administrators in the system and placed control of individual schools (everything from budgets to curriculum) into the hands of the principals, teachers, and parents. This ensured that each school was run by people who had a direct knowledge of a specific region in the district—and a personal interest in the system's overall success. School systems across America now use the SBM program.

Joseph A. Fernandez

Controversial Programs Lead to Downfall

Fernandez continued to streamline and to improve the New York City school system. When forced to make massive budget cuts, he refused to take away any services for students. Instead, he eliminated more administrative positions. But in 1991 his programs started to come under fire. That year he wanted to start an AIDS education program in high schools. Part of the program included passing out free condoms to students. Although some parents and administrators objected to the practice for religious reasons, Fernandez's program was eventually approved by the New York City Board of Education.

The following year Fernandez faced an even tougher battle over his Children of the Rainbow program, which offered elementary school students a new, multicultural curriculum. The program was designed to expose young people to all of the various ethnic groups and family situations in New York's rich cultural landscape. Fernandez wanted to encourage children to understand and respect peoples' racial and cultural differences—and to recognize the beauty of the city's "melting pot" atmosphere. His Children of the Rainbow program was considered controversial, though, because it also focused on families headed by homosexual couples. Many people in New York City thought Fernandez was putting too much emphasis on social issues and not enough on reading, writing, and arithmetic. Fernandez told Hiss in the *New Yorker,* "A lot of people call this a social agenda that's irrelevant to the three R's. But I think it's the fourth R—respect for yourself and others."

Nonetheless, anger over his ideas and his outspoken manner continued. In addition, the publication of his book *Tales Out of School* in early 1993 did little to help his cause. It criticized everyone from the mayor of New York City to the governor of the state for their stand on education. When Fernandez's contract ended in June of 1993, the New York City Board of Education voted 5-4 not to renew it.

Even though Fernandez was no longer chancellor of the city's school system, many of his reform programs were accepted and put into practice. The school board approved the creation of his numerous "community schools," which stay open late on weekdays and for six hours on Saturday, offering activities and classes for students. The schools also have free dental and medical clinics. Fernandez has no regrets about his tenure as chancellor. "I'm leaving here with my head held high," he told Barbara Kantrowitz of *Newsweek,* "and I can sleep well at night knowing that I did the best thing for the children of New York."

For Further Information

Fernandez, Joseph A., *Tales Out of School: Joseph Fernandez's Crusade to Rescue American Education,* Little, Brown, 1993.

Nation, May 10, 1993, pp. 631-36.

Newsweek, February 22, 1993, pp. 54-55.

New Yorker, April 12, 1993, pp. 43-54.

U.S. News & World Report, October 1, 1990, pp. 76-77.

Mary Joe Fernández

Professional tennis player
Born 1971, Dominican Republic

"I just decided that if I was going to go to school, I was going to do it right. And I wasn't ready to sacrifice being with my friends."

Mary Joe (María José) Fernández began playing professional tennis at the age of 14, but only part-time. Despite the lure of more money and quick fame, she chose to wear a neat uniform and attend Carrollton School of the Sacred Heart. She wanted to have normal high school experiences and spend some time with her friends. Fernández was an almost straight-A student throughout her high school years. During that time, she did manage to fit in a scaled-down schedule of tournaments, thus preparing herself to join the pro circuit in 1990.

Fernández was born in 1971 in the Dominican Republic to José and Sylvia Fernández. When she was six months old, her family moved to Miami, Florida. At age three she tagged along when her father and older sister went to play tennis. To keep the young Fernández occupied, her father gave her a tennis racket to bounce balls off a wall. Two years later she began taking lessons from a professional player.

Fernández showed talent right from the start. From the age of ten, she won one tournament after another, beginning with the United States Tennis Association Nationals.

Mary Joe Fernández

By the time she started high school, her coaches were pressuring her to turn professional and play full time. Many players do this in hopes of earning more money, reaching their full potential at an earlier age, and having a longer career.

Doesn't Want to Sacrifice Friendships

If she went pro, Fernández would have had to take correspondence courses by mail to complete her high school diploma. She would have had to fit in homework between practices, then fax it to her teachers from her hotel rooms. She decided to postpone the daily competition and travel until after she graduated. "I just decided that if I was going to go to school, I was going to do it right," Fernández explained to Austin Murphy of *Sports Illustrated*. "And I wasn't ready to sacrifice being with my friends."

When Fernández did miss classes to play in occasional tournaments, her friends helped out by faxing their class notes to her or dictating them to her over the phone. Because she was participating in the French Open at the time of her senior class final exams, her school allowed her to take them in August rather than in June. Unfortunately, she missed graduation ceremonies because of the tournament.

After collecting her diploma, Fernández jumped into the pro schedule full time in 1990. She did well, but soon discovered she had to make up for training time she had lost while in school. Although she won 40 of 50 singles matches and two tournaments, she suffered several injuries. During the year she was sidelined for a torn hamstring, a back injury, a severe knee sprain, and tendinitis. Her schoolmates had teased her for failing to pass the President's Council on Physical Fitness test in high school because she couldn't perform the "armhang" well enough. Her coaches believed her lack of stamina and injuries were due to her poor exercise program and weak upper body strength.

Fernández then hired a strength coach and started a consistent aerobic and training schedule. The hard work paid off. During the period between late 1990 and early 1991 she rose from seventh to fourth in the rankings of the top women players. In 1992 she reached the semifinals in the singles at the U.S. Open before losing to future champion Monica Seles. In the 1993 French Open, Fernández fought a courageous battle against Steffi Graf in the final before losing 6-4, 2-6, 4-6.

Olympic Moment

Fernández's brightest moment on the court, however, came in the 1992 Summer Olympics held in Barcelona, Spain. Fernández and doubles partner Gigi Fernández captured the gold medal by defeating Spain's own Arantxa Sánchez Vicaro and Conchita Martínez. Watching the match from the stands was Spanish King Juan Carlos.

By 1993 Fernández had earned more than $2 million from tournaments and endorsements (allowing companies to use her name to advertise their products). Despite her wealth and fame, Fernández continues to maintain a down-to-earth lifestyle and attitude. When Hurricane Andrew devastated areas of Florida in 1992, leaving many homeless, she helped organize a charity tournament to benefit the victims.

For Further Information

Sports Illustrated, February 11, 1991, pp. 76-79; June 14, 1993, pp. 26-33.

Tennis, June 1994, p. 94+.

World Tennis, February 1991, pp. 25-26.

Andy García

Actor
Born April 12, 1956, in Bejucal, Cuba

"There's nothing that I cherish more than my culture and what I am. But to call me the great Hispanic actor is ridiculous; it's racism. They don't call Dustin Hoffman the great Jewish-American actor."

Andy García

From a young age, Andy García had hopes of growing up to be a professional basketball player. When he was a senior in high school, however, he was benched for weeks after contracting mononucleosis. While recovering from the long-term illness, he began to think about a career in the entertainment industry. Although he had performed in several school plays, he never really considered acting as a profession. Once he made up his mind to pursue it, though, he never looked back. "From then on," he related to Jennet Conant in *Redbook,* "acting was a hunger in the pit of my stomach, and if I didn't cater to it, it got worse."

Andrés Arturo García Menendez was born in 1956 in Bejucal, Cuba, the youngest of three children. His mother, Amelie, taught English, while his father, Rene García Nuñez, was a prominent lawyer. The family enjoyed a comfortable life in the small town outside the capital city of Havana until the Cuban Revolution broke out in the late 1950s. Rebels led by Fidel Castro and Ernesto "Ché" Guevara sought to overthrow the brutal Cuban dictator Fulgencio Batista. After about two years of fighting, the rebels were victorious, and by December of 1959 Castro had risen to power. All private property was then seized by the new government. Having lost all they had, the García family fled to Miami.

García remembers his early years in Florida as difficult ones. He was only five when he came to America, and at that time he could speak no English. His parents took what work they could and began to rebuild life for the family. Even the children helped out. On his way home from school, young García picked up soda pop cans for change. When he grew older, he spent his evenings sweeping out the hosiery factory where his father worked.

Sports Give Way to Acting

Because he initially had trouble speaking English and was short for his age, García was involved in fights almost every day during his years in grade school. By the time he reached high school, however, his greatly improved English and his athletic abilities helped enlarge his social circle. After he became ill, though, García was forced to change his main goal in life. He took the switch from sports to acting in his stride. "Acting is very much like a game of basketball," he explained to Stephanie Mansfield in *Gentlemen's Quarterly*. "There's a moment-to-moment, spontaneous thing about it. You don't know what's going to happen."

García enrolled in Florida International University and majored in theater. He left college without graduating and soon found that Florida offered very few opportunities for a fledgling actor, so he moved to Los Angeles in 1978. While looking for acting parts, he worked at odd jobs—loading trucks and waiting on tables. When he could, García did improvisational comedy at clubs around Los Angeles. His first television role, a small part as a gang member, was on the premiere episode of the long-running television drama *Hill Street Blues* in 1981.

García found roles in motion pictures much harder to come by. Although he had

small parts in a few movies in the early 1980s, he was denied many more parts because of his ethnic background. As he told Mansfield, "I was rejected. And in the rudest of ways.... All the racist kinds of things." His first big film role finally came in 1985, when he played a Hispanic detective in *The Mean Season*.

Commands Attention with Breakthrough Role

The following year García landed the part of a charming but brutal drug dealer in *8 Million Ways to Die*. Although the movie received only lukewarm reviews, his performance stood out, capturing the attention of film critics—and of director Brian De Palma, who wanted García to play the villain in his next movie, *The Untouchables*. Fearing he would always be typecast as a Hispanic bad guy, García convinced De Palma to let him play a good guy FBI agent instead. His performance in the 1987 film won him international acclaim. Subsequent parts in films like *Black Rain* (with Michael Douglas) and *Internal Affairs* (with Richard Gere) also cast García in law enforcement roles, but he proved he was capable of acting out a range of intense emotions. And critics seemed to notice his presence in even small supporting roles in other feature films.

García achieved star status in 1990 with his appearance as the illegitimate nephew of Don Corleone in *The Godfather Part III*. He received an Academy Award nomination for his role and quickly went on to star in other major films, including *Hero,* with Dustin Hoffman and Geena Davis, and a thriller titled *Jennifer Eight*. Each of these films offered García the chance to branch out beyond the kinds of roles he had played almost exclusively earlier in his career: either a cop or a typically "ethnic" character of Hispanic descent. "There's nothing that I cherish more than my culture and what I am," García told Charla Krupp of *Glamour.* "But to call me the great Hispanic actor is ridiculous; it's racism. They don't call Dustin Hoffman the great Jewish-American actor."

In 1993 García moved behind the camera to direct a Spanish-language documentary film about Cuban musician Israel "Cachao" Lopez. In the future, he hopes to do a film about Cuba entitled *The Lost City.* Based on a work by Cuban novelist Guillermo Cabrera Infante, it will tell the story of a young man forced to leave Cuba at the time of the revolution. He will also star in two films: *Things to Do in Denver when You're Dead,* and *Steal Big, Steal Little.*

Family Comes First

In 1982 García married Marivi (short for Maria Victoria), a Cuban exile whom he met while in college. They have three daughters, and García insists that their lives remain very normal despite his stardom and wealth. He has a reputation for being a family man and has refused roles in films that include explicit sex scenes that might embarrass his family. To be near his family, he and his wife purchased a home in Key Biscayne, Florida, in 1991.

Part of the reason García moved back to Florida from Los Angeles is that he wanted his children to grow up in an environment that stresses their Cuban identity. He still considers himself a political exile of Cuba. "I had a great childhood in Miami Beach, but ultimately it's like having a stepmother,"

he explained to Conant. "If you are ripped from the womb of your real mother at the age of five, you can love your stepmother, but your mother is missing. You can't touch her, only love her from afar."

For Further Information

Gentlemen's Quarterly, December 1990, pp. 272-77+.
Glamour, January 1991, p. 92.
Hispanic, January/February 1994, pp. 14-16.
Redbook, January 1993, pp. 25-29.

Jerry Garcia

Singer, songwriter, guitarist
Born August 1, 1942, San Francisco, California

"It's just great to be involved in something that doesn't hurt anybody. If it provides some uplift and some comfort in people's lives, it's just that much nicer."

Jerry Garcia and his psychedelic 1960s band, the Grateful Dead, are enjoying a comeback in the 1990s. Along with other "classic rock" musicians, the Dead are recycling their hits, hitting the concert trail, and making new musical waves. Much of the reason for their success a second time around lies in the loyalty of their devoted, diehard fans—called Deadheads—who follow them all around the country.

Garcia was born in 1942 in San Francisco, California, to José and Ruth Garcia. His father was a Spanish immigrant who loved music. He owned a bar and was a

Jerry Garcia

respected musician and bandleader around San Francisco. The young Garcia had already begun piano lessons when his father died in a fishing accident in 1952. He gave up the piano shortly after this because of his lack of interest and a physical disfigurement (while chopping wood, his older brother had accidently cut off half of Garcia's right middle finger when Garcia was four).

Garcia's mother, who worked as a nurse, presented him with an accordion for his 15th birthday. By this time, however, he was more interested in owning a guitar. "So we took it down to the pawn shop and I got this little Danelectro, an electric guitar with a tiny amplifier, and, man, I was just in heaven," Garcia explained to a reporter for

Rolling Stone. "I stopped everything I was doing at the time."

Garcia had no interest in school, a problem that caused him to repeat the eighth grade. Matters didn't improve in high school. He cut classes and was regularly in trouble for fighting, drinking, and using drugs. When he was 17, he finally dropped out of school to join the army. Military discipline was no easier for him to accept. After nine months, he was discharged on the suggestion of his commander.

Learns Guitar in the Army

While in the army, Garcia had became interested in traditional American folk and blues music, and in acoustic guitar. "I used to do things like look at pictures of guitar players and look at their hands and try to make the chords they were doing, anything, any little thing," he said in *Rolling Stone.* For the next few years he practiced guitar and hung out with other young musicians who were crowding California college campuses. By 1964 he was part of a jug band called the Warlocks, which included Phil Lesh, Ron McKenna, Bill Kreutzmann, and Bob Weir. When the Beatles invaded American in 1964, the group turned to rock and roll.

Garcia and his bandmates fit right in with the San Francisco hippie culture. They performed at concerts throughout the state. Sometime during this period the band changed its name to the Grateful Dead and adopted a skull-and-roses logo. Warner Brothers offered them a recording contract in 1967, and the band issued its first album, *The Grateful Dead.*

Two more albums were released in the next two years, but neither one was a great success. Their first big seller was *Live Dead,* a 1969 recording of one of their live concerts. "Our income doesn't come from records," Garcia told the *Detroit Free Press.* "It comes from [live] work. Making records is a different thing. It's not playing for warm human beings…. In my mind, it's never really been making music."

Deadheads Keep Band Going

The 1970s brought tough times. After two successful albums were released in 1970, *Workingman's Dead* and *American Beauty,* McKenna died of alcohol abuse. The Dead broke away from Warner Brothers and embarked on a series of business ventures that were financial failures. They set up a headquarters in a small suburban house, then drifted apart. Garcia worked solo for a while. But Grateful Dead fans just wouldn't let the group die.

In its 1971 release, *Grateful Dead,* the group had inserted a short message: "Dead Freaks Unite. Who are you? Where are you? Send us your name and address and we'll keep you informed." The reaction was overwhelming. By 1972 there were newsletters that kept Deadheads in touch with the band and with each other.

The network is considerably more sophisticated now. Newsletters changed to telephone hotlines, which then gave way to electronic bulletin boards. The Deadhead mailing list contains 90,000 names in America and 20,000 in Europe. Deadheads come from a wide variety of professions and lifestyles—from college professors to bikers. Many buy concert tickets in packages and travel together from city to city following the band.

Nearly Killed by Drug Habit

Garcia's long-time drug abuse finally took its toll in 1985. That year he was arrested in Golden Gate Park in San Francisco and charged with possession of cocaine and heroin. Authorities allowed him to undergo drug rehabilitation treatment rather than serve time in jail. Despite this treatment, his physical condition continued to deteriorate. In 1986 he slipped into a week-long diabetic coma brought on by his drug use. He recovered, but his career was threatened. He had to take lessons to remember how to play guitar.

"There was something I needed or thought I needed from drugs," he explained to a *Rolling Stone* reporter. "I don't know what it was, exactly…. But after awhile, it was just the drugs running me, and that's an intolerable situation."

In 1987, with a healthy Garcia, the Grateful Dead released *In the Dark,* the group's first recording in seven years. The album became the group's biggest-selling record. One of the singles off the album, "Touch of Gray," became the Dead's first-ever hit. That year the Grateful Dead toured with folk legend Bob Dylan and on its own. Later in the year, Garcia played a two-week stint on Broadway.

Garcia continues to maintain a healthier lifestyle. Married twice, he is the father of four daughters. He continues to tour with the Grateful Dead, and their second-time success has made him wealthy. Regardless, he has not lost his 1960s outlook on life. "It's just great to be involved in something that doesn't hurt anybody," he told a *Rolling Stone* reporter. "If it provides some uplift and some comfort in people's lives, it's just that much nicer."

For Further Information

Detroit Free Press, June 19, 1984.

Jackson, Blair, *Grateful Dead: The Music Never Stopped,* Delilah Books, 1983.

New Yorker, October 11, 1993, pp. 96-102.

Rolling Stone, July 16, 1987; October 31, 1991, pp. 36-41+.

Gabriel García Márquez

Writer, journalist
Born March 6, 1928, Aracataca, Colombia

"I had an extraordinary childhood surrounded by highly imaginative and superstitious people, people who lived in a misty world populated by phantasms."

Gabriel García Márquez is one of Latin America's most influential writers. He writes best-sellers using "magic realism," a technique whereby fantastic happenings are interwoven with realistic, matter-of-fact events. His most acclaimed work is his 1967 novel, *Cien años de soledad* (published in English in 1970 as *One Hundred Years of Solitude*). For that masterpiece and for his entire body of writings, García Márquez was awarded the prestigious Nobel Prize for literature in 1982.

García Márquez was born in 1928 in Aracataca, Colombia, the oldest of 16 children born to Gabriel Eligio García Márquez and Luisa Santiaga Márquez Iguaran. He lived in the Caribbean part of Colombia, which he has described in interviews as a "fantastic place." The people there were descendants of pirates and smugglers and slaves, a mixture of cultures given to magical stories and legends. Because his family was poor, he lived with his grandparents until he was eight years old.

Childhood Filled with Ghosts

García Márquez grew very close to his grandparents. He claims his writing style comes from his grandmother, who would invent fantasies to avoid answering his questions about their life and its often sad realities. "I had an extraordinary childhood surrounded by highly imaginative and superstitious people," he explained to Manuel Osorio in the *UNESCO Courier,* "people who lived in a misty world populated by phantasms."

When his grandfather died in 1936, García Márquez was sent back to live with his parents. He found this change very disturbing at first. However, he soon realized that his parents were a positive influence for him. Raising many children in extreme poverty resulted in a hard life for his mother. Since García Márquez was the oldest child, his relationship with her was always very serious. He said later that there was nothing they could not tell each other. His father was a telegraph operator who wrote poetry, played the violin, and loved to read. He shared his love of the arts with his oldest son.

Free public schools are uncommon in much of South America. Since García Márquez's family was desperately poor, he had to apply for a scholarship to attend school when he was 12. To take a qualifying exam for the scholarship, he was forced to undertake a 700-mile, eight-day voyage by ship and train to the capital city of Bogotá. He was competing with

3,000 students for only 300 scholarships. While on the train, García Márquez met and befriended a shy man. It turned out that this man was in charge of the scholarship program. He awarded a scholarship to García Márquez, and his schooling was assured.

Journalism vs. Creative Writing

By the time García Márquez finished high school in 1946, he had earned the reputation of being a writer. Although he went on to study law at the University of Bogatá, he began to write short stories. In 1950 he joined the staff of a newspaper. During the day, he worked as a journalist. At night, he worked as a novelist. By 1955 he had completed work on his first book, *La hojarasca* ("Leaf Storm").

In 1958 García Márquez married his childhood sweetheart, Mercedes Barcha. After he had first proposed to her when he was 13, they maintained a sporadic, casual relationship until they were ready to marry. The couple eventually had two sons, Rodrigo and Gonzalo. García Márquez continued to work as a reporter, covering stories throughout Latin America, including the Cuban Revolution in 1959. His years as a reporter fueled his political perspective, but fiction-writing was his passion. By 1961 he had also managed to write two more books, *El coronel no tiene quien le escriba* ("No One Writes to the Colonel") and *La mala hora* ("The Evil Hour").

In 1965 García Márquez left journalism to write fiction full time. He spent 18 months in Mexico working on *One Hundred Years of Solitude*. When he finished the book, he was so poor he couldn't afford to

Gabriel García Márquez

mail it all at once to his publisher. To raise the money needed for postage, his wife sold their blender. She then divided the bundle of pages into two halves. By mistake she mailed the second half of the book first. Then, when she had raised more money, she sent along the first half. Luckily, the publisher recognized the excellence of the book, no matter in what order he received it.

Magical Masterpiece Is a Best-Seller

One Hundred of Years of Solitude is set in an imaginary community on the coast of Colombia and follows the lives of several generations of the Buendia family. Besides describing the complicated family relationships, the story reflects the political, social, and economic problems of South America. The mix of historical and fictitious elements in the book gives it its air of "magic realism."

The novel was a best-seller from the day it appeared in 1967. It has been translated into 30 languages and has sold more than ten million copies. *One Hundred Years of Solitude* has been so popular that García Márquez has been offered millions of dollars to permit a film version to be made of the book. He refuses to allow it. "I want readers to go on imagining the characters as they see them," he told *Playboy* interviewer Claudia Dreifus. "That isn't possible in the cinema. In movies, the image is so definite that the spectator can no longer imagine the character as he wants to, only as the screen imposes it on him."

During the 1960s and 1970s, works by Latin American writers were increasingly translated and made available to American readers. *One Hundred Years of Solitude* helped solidify the presence of these writers in the American market. A critic for the *Antioch Review,* quoted in *Hispanic Writers,* wrote that García Márquez's work would also help insure that "Latin America itself will be looked on less as a crazy subculture and more as a fruitful, alternative way of life."

García Márquez hasn't rested on his success. He has published numerous books—both fiction and nonfiction—and has written several screenplays for Spanish television. One of his other notable works is the 1985 novel *El amor en los tienpos del cólera* (published in English in 1988 as *Love in the Time of Cholera*). It is the captivating story of Florentino Ariza's undying love for the woman who has rejected him twice. Merle Rubin, writing in the *Christian Science Monitor,* labeled the novel "a boldly romantic, profoundly imaginative, fully imagined work of fiction that expands our sense of life's infinite possibilities."

Nobel Prize in Literature

When García Márquez was awarded the Nobel Prize in 1982, he was praised for his literary talents. The Swedish Academy that presents the prizes noted in its citation that "each new work of his is received by critics and readers as an event of world importance, is translated into many languages and published as quickly as possible in large editions."

The Academy also cited García Márquez for his activities on behalf of the poor and the oppressed in Latin America. The writer is a well-known social activist who uses his fame to promote political goals. García Márquez indicated that the money he received with the Nobel Prize would be used to help political prisoners and leftists in Latin America. His close friendship with Cuban President Fidel Castro and his political views eventually caused him to flee Colombia and settle in Mexico City, Mexico. The U.S. government has prohibited García Márquez from spending time in the United States because of his views and his involvement with Castro. Nonetheless, García Márquez has had a profound impact on Hispanic American literature, and his works continue to draw a large reading audience in the United States.

In the mid-1980s, García Márquez helped found and became the president of the Foundation for New Latin American Cinema, a film foundation and school in Havana, Cuba. It promotes all aspects of filmmaking in Latin America. In recent years, the foundation has tried to persuade international celebrities and film stars to lend their talent and money to its projects.

For Further Information

Christian Science Monitor, May 12, 1988.

Dolan, Sean, *Gabriel García Márquez,* Chelsea House, 1994.

Hispanic Writers, Gale, 1991, pp. 212-18.

Playboy, February 1983.

UNESCO Courier, October 1991, pp. 8-9.

Roberto C. Goizueta

Chairman and chief executive officer of
   Coca-Cola
Born November 18, 1931, Havana, Cuba

"We are not going to spend long hours sitting down and trying to foretell the future. Instead, we will devote our energies to creating it."

When Roberto C. Goizueta became the chief executive officer (CEO) of the Coca-Cola Company in March of 1981, the 95-year-old beverage company was worth about $4 billion. At the time, only one cola—the original—carried the name Coca-Cola. Throughout the 1980s, Goizueta streamlined the company's operations while introducing new products to worldwide markets. By the early 1990s, with over half a dozen Coca-Cola products being sold in more than 195 countries around the world, the company had grown to more than $50 billion in value. Despite these achievements, Goizueta is not content to let the company rest. "We are not going to spend long hours

sitting down and trying to foretell the future," he told *Financial World.* "Instead, we will devote our energies to creating it."

Goizueta was born in 1931 in Havana, Cuba, to Crispulo Goizueta and Aida Cantera. His father owned a sugar plantation and was wealthy enough to send him to a small preparatory school in New Hampshire. There young Goizueta learned to speak English partly by watching movies. After he graduated as class valedictorian, he attended Yale University in New Haven, Connecticut, to study chemical engineering. He received his bachelor of science degree in 1953, shortly before marrying Olga Casteleiro. The couple eventually had three children. Goizueta returned to Cuba in 1954, but instead of working on his family's sugar plantation, he became the technical director of Coca-Cola's plant in Havana.

Future Altered by the Cuban Revolution

The Goizueta family's circumstances were soon changed by a social revolution that swept across Cuba. At the time, the country was controlled by Fulgencio Batista, considered by many to be the most brutal dictator in Latin America. A rebel force led by Fidel Castro and Ernesto "Ché" Guevara tried to overthrow Batista. After a few years, the rebels' guerrilla warfare—consisting of quick attacks and ambushes—proved successful, and Castro and his comrades took over the government in 1959. They immediately put banks and other businesses under the control of the government. They also seized the land of wealthy landowners, and Goizueta's family lost all of its money. In 1960 Goizueta fled to Miami, Florida.

Roberto C. Goizueta

Coca-Cola soon made Goizueta an assistant to the senior vice president in charge of research for Latin America. He was based in Nassau, the capital of the Bahamas. In 1964 the company transferred him to its corporate headquarters in Atlanta, Georgia. Over the next 15 years, he steadily climbed the corporate ladder. By 1980 he had become Coca-Cola's president and chief operating officer.

Coca-Cola's chief executive officer at the time was Paul Austin. Although Coca-Cola was still the number one soft drink company in the world—selling over 1.3 billion cases of Coke a year—Austin had failed to make the company grow. Coca-Cola's share of the soft drink market was gradually declining. Robert Woodruff, the long-term corporate executive who had built Coca-Cola into a powerful firm and who was still the chairman of the company's executive committee, decided a change

was necessary. In 1981, he called Goizueta into his office and asked him, as John Huey related in *Fortune,* "Roberto, how would you like to run my company?" Goizueta is said to have responded, "Well, Mr. Woodruff, I'd be flattered."

Takes Gambles and Wins

The Coca-Cola Company seemed to bounce back as soon as Goizueta took over its top position. He did what no previous executive of the company had dared to do: he took risks. In an effort to focus Coca-Cola's interests primarily on the soft drink market, Goizueta sold off several unrelated businesses the company owned. He also gambled on brand development, making the decision to offer the calorie-conscious public a diet cola worthy of the Coca-Cola label.

Diet Coke was introduced in 1982, and many industry observers were sure it would fail. If it did, then the Coca-Cola name, which had been on only one product for nearly a century, would be dragged down with it. But the gamble paid off. Within a few years, Diet Coke became the world's third most popular soft drink (behind original Coke and its archrival, Pepsi). By 1986 the company's sales of Coca-Cola, Diet Coke, Cherry Coke, Diet Cherry Coke, Caffeine-Free Coke, and Caffeine-Free Diet Coke had reached more than 2.2 billion cases per year.

New Coke Is a Disaster

The introduction of New Coke (called simply "Coke") in 1985 was an idea that never took off—and almost cost the company its lead in the soft drink war against

Pepsi. Goizueta thought it was important for Coca-Cola to come out with a sweeter-tasting cola to compete with Pepsi's growing popularity. But consumer complaints about changes to the 100-year-old original cola formula were immediate and loud. Just three months after New Coke hit the shelves, Goizueta had to admit he had made a mistake. The original-formula Coke was then brought back as Coke Classic, and it quickly regained its top spot among soft drinks.

Another gamble that almost didn't pay off for Coca-Cola was its purchase of Columbia Pictures in 1982 for $692 million. The beverage company had no experience in managing a movie studio, and Columbia had a long string of box office losers after the hit movie *Ghostbusters* was released in 1984. But Goizueta had also used Columbia to invest in television programs, such as game show favorites *Wheel of Fortune* and *Jeopardy.* The money made through those shows quickly offset the money lost by the movies. In 1989 Coca-Cola sold its share in Columbia Pictures to the Sony Corporation for $1.55 billion.

"We used to be an American company with a large international business," Goizueta remarked to Huey in *Fortune.* "Now we are a large international company with a sizable American business." With the fall of communist regimes throughout Eastern Europe in the late 1980s and the early 1990s, the worldwide soft drink market opened up. Coca-Cola was there, investing $1 billion in the region. It helped build million-dollar bottling plants in cities such as Warsaw, Poland, and St. Petersburg, Russia. And in 1993 Coca-Cola's name was on four of the five top-selling soft drinks in the world.

Goizueta has managed the Coca-Cola Company through one of the most successful periods in its history. In April of 1994, the company's board of directors convinced him to continue working for Coca-Cola even after he turns 65 in November of 1996, the date he was originally scheduled to retire.

For Further Information

Barron's, May 9, 1994, pp. 29-33.
Business Week, April 13, 1992, pp. 96, 98.
"Coca-Cola," *Encyclopedia of Consumer Brands,* Volume 1: *Consumable Products,* edited by Janice Jorgensen, Gale, 1994.
The Chronicle of Coca-Cola Since 1886, Time, Inc., 1950.
Financial World, April 4, 1989, p. 78.
Fortune, October 26, 1987, pp. 46-56; May 31, 1993, pp. 44-54.
Wall Street Journal, April 22, 1994, p. B12.

Henry Barbosa Gonzalez

U.S. congressman
Born May 3, 1916, San Antonio, Texas

"If a bill violates the constitutional rights of even one person, then it has to be struck down."

H enry Gonzalez, Democratic congressman from Texas, was the first Mexican American elected to the U.S. Congress. Now nearly 80 years old, he won his first political election in 1953 when he ran

Henry Barbosa Gonzalez

for San Antonio's city council. Three years later he became the first Mexican American in over 100 years to be elected to the Texas state senate. In 1961 he began his service in the House of Representatives in Washington D.C. Over the years, his fiery speeches against what he saw as corruption or evil in government have brought him much attention. Those members of Congress who disagree with his stand have often labeled him an eccentric or a stubborn fool. No one, however, has ever questioned his reputation for honesty and independence.

Henry Barbosa Gonzalez was born in 1916 into a family that traces its roots in Mexico back hundreds of years. In the sixteenth century his ancestors voyaged from southern Spain to help settle the northern

Mexican state of Durango. In the early 1900s, his father, Leonides Gonzalez, was mayor of the town of Mapimi in Durango. He and his wife, Genoveva Barbosa, were forced to flee to San Antonio during the 1911 Mexican Revolution, which pitted farm peasants against wealthy landowners and the Mexican government.

While Gonzalez was growing up, he was surrounded by political talk. His close-knit family also stressed education, and the young Gonzalez became an avid reader, spending many hours at the local library. After attending San Antonio public schools, he enrolled in San Antonio Junior College, studying there for two years. He then entered the University of Texas at Austin to study engineering and law. Short on money, he had to return to his hometown after only two years. He eventually earned his law degree in 1943 from St. Mary's University School of Law in San Antonio.

Gonzalez did not begin his career as a lawyer. Instead, he ran a Spanish-English translation service and worked as a probation officer in the county's juvenile court system. In 1950 he began working for the San Antonio Housing Authority. As part of his job, he helped resettle families into new homes after they had been evicted from their previous ones.

Elected to First Office

In 1953 Gonzalez entered the world of politics, winning a seat on San Antonio's city council. One of the laws he helped enact during his term ended segregation in city buildings. Three years later he became the first Mexican American Texas state senator in 110 years. He attracted national attention as an outspoken defender of equal rights for minorities. At one point, he spoke on the floor of the Texas senate for 22 continuous hours against 13 bills he thought were racist. He told Christopher Hitchens of *Harper's* magazine years later, "If a bill violates the constitutional rights of even one person, then it has to be struck down."

In 1960 Gonzalez was elected to Congress for the first time, as a Democrat representing the Twentieth Congressional District. Again, he broke new ground, becoming the first Mexican American congressman from Texas. Although his district is mainly Hispanic, Gonzalez's work in Congress has been for people in all ethnic groups. As Carlos Conde noted in *Hispanic,* Gonzalez "believes that using ethnicity as a crutch only invites more typecasting."

Witness to Recent Events in American History

Reelected by overwhelming margins to every term since, Gonzalez has seen many events that have become part of American history. In 1963 he rode with President John F. Kennedy on Air Force One (the president's plane) just minutes before Kennedy was assassinated in Dallas. In 1972 he wanted to question President Richard Nixon's administration about its possible role in the burglary of the Democratic national headquarters in the Watergate apartment complex. He was denied the chance. The Watergate Scandal brought down the Nixon presidency in 1974. And in the mid-1970s, he tried to bring attention to the safety problems surrounding nuclear plants. In 1979 the Three Mile Island nuclear plant in Pennsylvania suffered a partial melting of its uranium core, releasing

some radioactivity into the surrounding land and water.

Gonzalez has ruffled a few feathers in Congress and in the White House with his views over the years. He considers himself a moderate in the fight for Mexican American civil rights and opposes radical militants. Still, he has fought for many Mexican American goals, including protection for farm workers, better education and housing for the poor, and the defeat of the bracero program (recruitment of Mexican laborers by U.S. agents).

Gonzalez's reputation as an eccentric stems from several causes: his fondness for wearing "electric blue" suits; his habit of delivering very long, rambling speeches; and his tendency to wait until evening to deliver those speeches to a mostly empty House chamber. Still, his speeches always seem to correctly predict scandals lurking just ahead. Even though few members of Congress bother to stay around to listen, Gonzalez knows that a cable television network is broadcasting every minute of his speech to the American people who tune in.

Battles Two Presidents

During the 1980s, Gonzalez fought against President Ronald Reagan and his administration. Gonzalez tried unsuccessfully to have the administration fund programs to build more low-cost housing. He also attacked Reagan for intervening in the affairs of other countries and for abusing the power of the presidency. Gonzalez called for Reagan's impeachment in 1983 after the United States invaded Granada. In 1987 he again wanted Reagan impeached for his possible involvement in the arms-for-hostages scandal involving Iran.

In 1988 Gonzalez was named chairman of the powerful House Committee on Banking, Finance, and Urban Affairs. His committee helped find a remedy for the failing savings and loans associations across the country in the late 1980s. Gonzalez showed his independence from the politics of Washington when he brought about a formal investigation of five senators who might have had improper dealings with people involved in the savings-and-loan scandal. Four of those five senators were Democrats.

In January 1991 Gonzalez again called for the impeachment of a president, this time of George Bush. That month the United States entered into the Persian Gulf War with Iraq over its invasion of Kuwait. Gonzalez believed Bush did not rightly seek permission from Congress to wage the war. He also tried to show that the Bush administration had sold weapons to Saddam Hussein, the Iraqi president, months before the war.

Although mocked by some of his fellow members of Congress and unsuccessful in his attempts to impeach two recent presidents, Gonzalez remains committed to his ideal—serving the people who have elected him. Hitchens quoted Wisconsin Republican Toby Roth as saying, "[Gonzalez] has the stick-to-it-iveness of an English bulldog. He's a genuine old-fashioned public servant."

For Further Information

Harper's, October 1992, pp. 84-96.
Hispanic, October 1989, pp. 13-14.
Nation, June 1, 1992, pp. 740-41.
New York Times, March 24, 1994, p. A18.

Juan Gonzalez

Professional baseball player
Born October 16, 1969, Vega Baja, Puerto Rico

"When my playing days are over, I will be focused on serving the people of Puerto Rico, not from a political platform but from a social platform."

The children of Puerto Rico call baseball superstar Juan Gonzalez their hero. He grew up hitting bottlecaps with a broomstick bat and, at a young age, went on to become major league baseball's home run champion in 1992 and 1993. He spends the off-season visiting Puerto Rican schools to speak to children. After his baseball career ends, he plans a career in social work.

Gonzalez was born in 1969 in Puerto Rico. He was raised in an area called Alto de Cuba—a tough neighborhood where the narrow streets are now filled with crime, abandoned houses, drugs, and poverty. Shopkeepers there remember the young, barefoot Gonzalez playing baseball in those streets. Today Gonzalez deplores the condition of his old barrio (Spanish-speaking neighborhood). When he can, he tries to encourage the children there to escape as he has.

"It makes me feel bad and sad at the same time," he related to Tom Verducci in *Sports Illustrated.* "The youth is losing its future to drugs. But I also blame the government authorities for not caring for the people of the barrio. There is not a baseball field or a basketball court for them."

Signs with Rangers at 16

When Gonzalez was 13, his father, a high school math teacher, moved the family to a safer neighborhood. Here he played baseball on organized teams. His coaches immediately recognized his remarkable talent for hitting home runs. When Gonzalez was 16, a scout from the Texas Rangers offered him a professional baseball contract worth $75,000. His father had to sign it because Gonzalez was still underage.

Gonzalez weighed only 170 pounds when he started with the Rangers, and he spent his first seasons playing on their minor league teams. He began lifting weights to increase his strength. Late in the 1989 season, he was brought up from the minors and hit his first major league home run. He was 19 years old. The next year, his first full season in the big leagues, he smashed 27 homers.

In 1992 Juan hit 43 home runs and drove in 109 runs, capturing the major league home run title. When he flew home to Puerto Rico after the season ended, five thousand fans met him at the airport in San Juan. One hundred thousand more lined the road he took to his hometown. The people love him because of his success and because he hasn't forgotten his roots. "Juan Gonzalez is the perfect guy that, if I was a youngster, I'd want to emulate," Hall of Fame pitcher Jim Palmer said, as quoted by *Washington Post* reporter David Mills. "He hasn't been caught for speeding. He hasn't taken a gun through a metal detector. He's done everything he possibly can to be the best player he can, and also be a responsible citizen."

Juan Gonzalez

Has High Social Concerns

Gonzalez took this responsibility to heart. He believed it was his duty to be a role model for the youth of Puerto Rico and to help the people of his neighborhood. He paid electric, water, and medical bills for the needy in Alto de Cuba. He bought vitamins for the boys who worked out with him in the neighborhood gym. He treated residents of the neighborhood to a Christmas party in the streets. During the off-season, he visited more than 50 Puerto Rican schools. He signed autographs and talked to students, encouraging them to avoid drugs and to stay in school.

The children of Puerto Rico called Gonzalez "Igor," a nickname he earned at age 10 when his hero was a professional wrestler called "The Mighty Igor." They lined up for his autograph and imitated his lifestyle. When not playing baseball, Gonzalez lived with his parents, and resumed his own education. In 1992 he began taking English lessons. Since Spanish is his native tongue, he needed an interpreter to help him with questions from American reporters. Some sports writers say his inability to speak English helped him avoid unwanted interviews and publicity.

Gonzalez is a fierce competitor who hates to strike out. He has been criticized for throwing his bat and helmet when his hitting has been off. After a strong 1993 season, in which he hit 46 home runs, Gonzalez started the 1994 season poorly. By mid-June he was hitting only .258. He claimed to be hampered by a number of injuries, but many people felt these injuries were not that serious. However, by the time the season came to an early end in August because of the players' strike, Gonzalez had raised his average to .275 and had batted in 85 runs.

Even with his career on the rise, the muscle-bound power hitter had definite post-baseball plans. "When my playing days are over, I will be focused on serving the people of Puerto Rico, not from a political platform but from a social platform," he told Verducci. "God gave me a good mind and the ability to succeed in baseball. I understand that I have to give back for what God has given me."

For Further Information

Sport, May 1993, p. 61+.
Sports Illustrated, April 5, 1993, p. 60+; June 13, 1994, pp. 74-75.
Washington Post, August 23, 1993, p. B1.

Rodolfo "Corky" Gonzalez

Chicano leader, writer, boxer
Born June 18, 1929, Denver, Colorado

Gonzalez's epic poem I Am Joaquín *had a tremendous social influence, uniting Mexican American youths in their own quest for identity.*

Rodolfo "Corky" Gonzalez is a dynamic and colorful personality whose interests range from boxing to poetry to politics. He played a large part in the Chicano movement of the late 1960s and early 1970s. (The word "Chicano" comes from Mechicano, the same Nahuatl, or ancient Aztec, word from which the country of Mexico derived its name.) Young Mexican Americans involved in the Chicano movement not only struggled for civil rights but also sought to understand their cultural roots. To help provide his people with a sense of identity, Gonzalez wrote *I Am Joaquín / Yo Soy Joaquín.* Many people consider this work the classic epic poem of the Chicano movement.

Gonzalez was born in a barrio (a Spanish-speaking neighborhood) of Denver, Colorado, to a poor family of migrant workers. While growing up, he attended public schools in Denver. In the springs and summers of his youth, he worked alongside family members in the Colorado sugar beet fields. Before graduating from high school, Gonzalez became interested in boxing as a way to earn extra money and escape farm work. His boxing skills developed quickly

Rodolfo "Corky" Gonzalez

and, while still a teenager, he became a Golden Gloves winner. He began his professional boxing career in 1947 and went on to win 65 of his 75 matches. Before he quit the ring, he was ranked as a contender for the World Featherweight title.

Gonzalez left boxing in the late 1950s and ran a neighborhood bar full time. He soon turned his attention to politics. In 1957 he became the first Mexican American chosen to be district captain of the Denver Democratic party. Three years later he coordinated the John F. Kennedy presidential campaign in Colorado.

Tries to Help Mexican American Youths

Gonzalez was greatly disturbed by the poor conditions under which Mexican Americans lived in the Southwest. He was especially concerned with Mexican American youths and their seemingly unjust treatment by government officials and police officers. In 1963, hoping to solve some of these problems, Gonzalez organized Los Voluntarios ("The Volunteers"), a group that fought to give Mexican Americans a greater political voice. Over the next few years, he also helped direct anti-poverty and youth employment programs in Denver.

In 1966, however, a Denver newspaper published an article accusing Gonzalez of discriminating against African Americans and whites in the youth program. Angered over the accusation, Gonzalez resigned from the boards of the government programs and left the Democratic party.

Gonzalez was still determined to help young Mexican Americans but refused to do so through standard political organizations. Instead, he developed an organization called the Crusade for Justice in 1967 to raise political and ethnic awareness among Chicano youths and to help in the fight for their civil rights. The following year he converted an old school and church building in Denver into a Crusade school, theater, gym, nursery, and cultural center. The school was named after the ancient Aztec city of Tlatelolco, located near the Aztec capital of Tenochtitlán (now Mexico City). In addition to offering classes from kindergarten through the twelfth grade, the Crusade school taught students about the cultures of their Spanish and native Mexican ancestors.

Writes "I Am Joaquín"

It was during this time that Gonzalez wrote his long poem *I Am Joaquín / Yo Soy Joaquín.* In the poem, the hero Joaquín journeys into the past to view and take part in important events in Aztec, Mexican, and Mexican American history. The journey is both historical and spiritual. As Joaquín travels back to the present, he comes to terms with who he is. Gonzalez's epic poem had a tremendous social influence, uniting Mexican American youths in their own quest for identity. *I Am Joaquín,* written in both English and Spanish, was read aloud at rallies, performed as a drama by street theaters, and was even made into a film by leading Mexican American director Luis Valdez (see **Luis Valdez**).

In the summer of 1968, the Crusade for Justice took part in the historic Poor People's March on Washington, D.C. Here Gonzalez announced the "Plan of the Barrio," which demanded improved education, housing, and land reform for Mexican Ameri-

cans. The following year the Crusade for Justice sponsored the first national Chicano Youth Liberation Conference in Denver. The main theme of the conference was cultural identity and pride. At the end of five days, participants produced a document titled *El Plan Espiritual de Aztlán* ("The Spiritual Plan of Aztlán"; Aztlán is the mythical home of the Aztec.) The conference members declared that the American Southwest would be the new Aztlán, a new cultural home for Mexican Americans.

Forms Political Party for Mexican Americans

In 1970, at the next Chicano Youth Liberation Conference, Gonzalez formed the Colorado La Raza Unida ("United Race") party to help elect Mexican Americans to political office in the state. His political ideas soon spread as the party sprang up in other states. However, at a national convention of La Raza Unida in 1972 in El Paso, Texas, Gonzalez lost his bid to become the party's permanent chairperson.

Gonzalez then returned to Denver to continue his work with the Crusade for Justice. He supported the drive for Mexican American rights and the efforts of César Chávez (see **César Chávez**) to organize a union for Mexican American migrant farm workers in California. As the 1970s wore on, though, Gonzalez's influence on the national level declined.

In the late 1970s, while remaining head of the Crusade for Justice, Gonzalez became involved again in boxing, this time helping to train amateurs. He turned his attention to professional boxers a few years later. In 1987, however, Gonzalez was involved in a serious automobile accident. His recovery was slow and his work with young Mexican Americans was hampered as a result of his injuries, but his overall impact on the fight for Chicano rights remains unquestionable.

For Further Information

Gonzalez, Rodolfo, *I Am Joaquín / Yo Soy Joaquín,* Bantam, 1972.

Marín, Christine, *A Spokesman of the Mexican American Movement: Rodolfo "Corky" Gonzales and the Fight for Chicano Liberation, 1966-1972,* R and E Research Associates, 1977.

Steiner, Stan, *La Raza: The Mexican Americans,* Harper and Row, 1969, pp. 378-92.

Antonia Hernández

MALDEF president and general counsel
Born May 30, 1948, Coahuila, Mexico

"The 1990s is a threshold decade. We need to move. Otherwise we'll develop into a community with a small middle class and a large poverty class."

As president of the Mexican American Legal Defense and Educational Fund (MALDEF), Antonia Hernández is an advocate (defender and spokesperson) for the nation's large and growing Hispanic community. Her opinions and advice on how legal or educational issues affect Hispanics in the United States are featured in newspapers and magazines and on radio and television talk shows across the country.

Antonia Hernández

MALDEF is an organization that attempts to support and defend Hispanic Americans. As its president, Hernández attempts to correct any discrimination against her people through negotiation, compromise, or legal action. Her special areas of concern are immigrant rights, employment discrimination, unequal education opportunities, and voting and language rights.

Hernández was born in the Mexican state of Coahuila in the town of Torreón in 1948. When she was eight, her family immigrated to the United States, settling in East Los Angeles, California. Her father, Manuel, was a gardener and laborer. Her mother, Nicolasa, was a homemaker who raised six children and worked odd jobs whenever possible. As the oldest child, Hernández was often called upon to watch over her younger brothers and sisters. "I grew up in a very happy environment but a very poor environment," Hernández told an interviewer for *Parents* magazine.

Hernández credits her early upbringing in Mexico with instilling pride in her Mexican roots. "When I came to the United States, I was very proud of who I was," she told the *Los Angeles Daily Journal*. "I was a Mexican. I had an identity. I had been taught a history, a culture of centuries of rich civilization so I had none of the psychoses [mental disorders] of people who don't know who they are."

Wants to Follow a Noble Profession

Hernández's parents taught their children that working for the public good was a noble thing to do. Hernández was working toward a postgraduate degree in education when she decided she could be more useful to her community with a law degree. She already had a bachelor's degree and a teaching certificate from the University of California at Los Angeles (UCLA). She realized that she could help children more by changing the laws she believed were holding them back.

Hernández's professors encouraged her to attend Harvard University, but she chose to remain at UCLA so she could be near her family. Since her parents were sacrificing to help her with school costs, she felt it would be best to stay at home and help them with the rest of the family when she had the time.

Hernández was not a straight-A student in law school, but her professors remember her as bright and well-spoken. She was respected for being able to make her point

without angering others. She explained that she cared more about her organizations and issues than earning top grades. During law school she worked for several Chicano (Mexican American) student organizations. She wanted to be a well-rounded person and intended to work in public service law. She received her law degree in 1974.

Hernández's first job as a lawyer was for the East Los Angeles Center for Law and Justice. She handled criminal and civil cases, which often involved police brutality. She went on to direct a Legal Aid Foundation office where she helped defend those who did not have enough money to hire a lawyer. She also fought for the passage of state laws that would help minorities and the poor.

In 1977 Hernández married Michael Stern, a fellow lawyer. The following year, she was offered a job as an attorney for the United States Senate Judiciary Committee. While in Washington, D.C., she gained valuable experience. She helped write laws and advised government officials on immigration and human-rights issues.

The time spent in Washington, D.C., also gave Hernández a broader understanding of the diversity within the U.S. Hispanic community. She came to know the problems facing Cuban Americans, Puerto Rican Americans, and other Hispanic groups. Since that time, she has sought to increase cooperation among civil rights groups across both racial and ethnic lines. The key to doing this, she believes, is through education. "We don't know ourselves," Hernández explained to Roger E. Hernandez in *Hispanic*. "For instance, we Mexican Americans have to understand the Puerto Rican experience, the Cuban experience. We don't have a good enough grasp about these things."

Begins Working for MALDEF

In 1980 MALDEF asked Hernández to join their staff. She has worked for the organization ever since, serving as its president and general counsel since 1985. Her experiences growing up as an immigrant in Los Angeles have helped her to understand the special present-day problems of Hispanics in the United States. For example, her difficulties learning English while attending public schools in Los Angeles have made her an effective defender of bilingual education (education in an English-language school system in which minority students with little fluency in English are taught in their native language).

Community involvement is important to Hernández. She continues to work for a number of organizations, including the Quality Education for Minorities Network and the Latino Museum of History, Art, and Culture. After the 1992 riots in Los Angeles in the wake of the Rodney King court decision (a not-guilty verdict for four white police officers who were videotaped while savagely beating King, an African American motorist), Los Angeles Mayor Tom Bradley appointed Hernández to a commission to oversee the reconstruction of the city.

Hernández felt it was extremely important for Hispanics to be involved in the rebuilding process. She saw it as an opportunity for Hispanics to begin changing the way their community has been viewed in the United States. "The 1990s is a threshold decade," Hernández told a *Hispanic* interviewer. "We need to move. Otherwise we'll develop into a community with a small middle class and a large poverty class."

For Further Information

Hispanic, December 1990. pp. 17-18; September 1991, pp. 18-22.
Los Angeles Daily Journal, September 3, 1985, p. 1.
Parents, March 1985, pp. 96-100+.
Vista, August 1992, pp. 6, 28.

Guillermo (Willie) Hernandez

Former professional baseball player
Born November 14, 1954, Aguada, Puerto Rico

"A lot of people make mistakes. I believe I made a good mistake."

Guillermo Hernandez was a left-handed relief pitcher who was known in the world of baseball for working only the last couple innings of a game, often when the game was on the line. In baseball jargon, he was known as a "stopper" or "short man." In 1984, Hernandez recorded 32 saves in 33 appearances, an almost unheard of statistic. That year he helped the Detroit Tigers to victory in the World Series. He was named the Most Valuable Player in the American League and was honored with the Cy Young Award as the league's best pitcher. Few pitchers in baseball history have had so successful a season.

Hernandez was born in 1954 in Aguada, Puerto Rico. He was the youngest of nine children born to his father, a sugarcane worker, and his mother, a housekeeper. While growing up, he did odd jobs to help his family. "My

Guillermo (Willie) Hernandez

Even though Hernandez's team eventually lost 1-0, he pitched seven scoreless innings. His career on the mound was underway. After pitching with his team for a month and a half, he traveled to Italy as a member of the Puerto Rican national team. They beat the United States for the first time, but lost the championship to Japan.

Major League Career Starts Slowly

In 1974 the Philadelphia Phillies signed Hernandez to a professional contract, but kept him on their minor league team for three seasons. The Chicago Cubs then drafted him during the winter of 1976. The following season marked his rookie year in the majors. For most players, making the majors is the end of a long and difficult journey, but Hernandez felt his troubles were only beginning.

As a reliever for the Cubs, Hernandez never had more than four saves during each of his first five seasons. "People were talking behind my back, saying I'm through," Hernandez told a reporter for the *Detroit Free Press*. He felt he was not appreciated in Chicago and was always in the shadow of more well-known pitchers. By 1981 he was back to the minors. He finished the season with a losing record and a bad attitude.

In 1982 Hernandez asked the Cubs for a release. They granted his wishes by trading him to the Philadelphia Phillies. In a new city and with a new organization, his pitching improved. With his first winning season since 1978 (he finished the year 8-4), he helped Philadelphia to the World Series. Even though the Phillies eventually lost to the Baltimore Orioles, Hernandez ended the

parents would buy me things," he related to a reporter for the *Detroit Free Press,* "but I could help pay for the bills."

Hernandez played baseball from a young age, although he started out as a rarity in the sport—a left-handed third baseman. It was an accident that he soon became a pitcher. As a teenager he played semiprofessional ball on Sundays. The day before the game, he would often pitch batting practice to his team. "I got a good fastball and a good breaking ball," he told a *Detroit Free Press* reporter. "But I [didn't] know how to pitch. One time, somebody got suspended, somebody else got hurt. We [didn't] have a pitcher. My manager [gave] me the ball."

season on a good note: he signed a three-year contract worth $1.7 million.

Carries Tigers to a Banner Year

Hernandez's performances caught the attention of the Detroit Tigers. For three years they tried to trade for him, but were unsuccessful. Finally, during the last week of spring training in 1984, Philadelphia agreed to a trade and Hernandez put on a Tigers uniform.

1984 was a banner year for the Detroit Tigers. They won 35 of their first 40 games—a major league record. The team also accomplished the rare feat of spending the entire season in first place. One of the main reasons for the team's success was Hernandez. His late inning trips to the mound were a familiar sight. Batters dreaded seeing the 6-foot-2, 185-pound pitcher with the menacing look and macho mustache. His walk from the bullpen became a sure sign that the Tigers were going to win.

Hernandez had a terrific season in 1984. In addition to his 32 saves, he compiled a 9-3 record with 112 strikeouts and a 1.92 earned-run average. But even though he helped win the World Series, collected numerous awards, and had a contract that ran through the following season, he was dissatisfied. He threatened to leave the club unless he was given a new contract worth more money. He negotiated with team officials for three months. Finally, in January 1985, the Detroit Tigers offered him a baseball contract worth more than $1 million a year, the richest contract in Tiger history to that point.

Problems with the Media

During the late 1980s Hernandez encountered some difficulties in dealing with the media. During 1988 spring training, he dumped a bucket of ice water on *Detroit Free Press* sports columnist Mitch Albom, who had written articles criticizing Hernandez. He later apologized for the incident, but only half-heartedly. "A lot of people make mistakes," he was quoted as saying by *Sports Illustrated.* "I believe I made a good mistake."

That same year Hernandez asked fans and writers to call him Guillermo instead of Willie (the name he had previously used in his baseball career). He explained that he wanted to show respect for his ethnic roots by returning to his Latin name. He pitched well that year, but it was to be his last successful season.

Hernandez injured his elbow late in the 1989 season and had to have surgery in September of that year. The Tigers then released him. A month later, he signed a contract with the Senior Professional Baseball Association. In the spring of 1990, the Oakland Athletics picked him up, but released him shortly afterward. His arm had never fully recovered from the injury. His pitching days over, he retired to Puerto Rico to live with his wife and two sons.

For Further Information

Detroit Free Press, March 26, 1984; August 26, 1984; January 10, 1985.
Sporting News, March 5, 1990, pp. 23-24.
Sports Illustrated, March 14, 1988, p. 14.

Carolina Herrera

Fashion designer
Born 1939, Caracas, Venezuela

"I am never satisfied. I'm a perfectionist. When I see the show is ready and the collection is out and they're quite nice, I still say, 'I could do much better.'"

Carolina Herrera is one of the most respected fashion designers in the United States. Born to a wealthy South American family, she was a member of fashionable society even as a child. She began her business in 1981 at the insistence of friends and business people who admired the elegant clothes she designed for herself. Since that time she has dressed some of the world's most famous women.

Maria Carolina Josefina Pacanins y Nino (her full Spanish name) was born in Caracas, Venezuela, in 1939. She was the daughter of Guillermo Pacanins, who served as an officer in the Venezuelan Air Force and, later, as the governor of Caracas. Her parents enjoyed hosting lavish parties in their glamorous homes and loved to wear the latest fashions. As a young girl, Carolina designed clothes for her dolls. As she grew older, she began to design them for herself and her friends.

When Herrera married her childhood friend Reinaldo Herrera, she found even more reason to dress glamorously. Her mother-in-law, who was a wealthy sponsor of artists, owned an enormous, historic house in Caracas that had been built in 1590. Herrera dressed herself to fit in with her new elegant surroundings. She first made the annual Best Dressed List in 1971 and has not been off it since. Ten years later she won a spot in the Fashion Hall of Fame.

Hobby Turns into a Career

Herrera and her husband had four daughters—Mercedes, Ana Luisa, Carolina, and Patricia. She began her professional career in 1981 when her children were grown and she wanted to try something new. "I have always liked fashion," Herrera told Mary Batts Estrada in *Hispanic,* "and I thought I was capable of doing it, so I said, 'Why not try it?'"

By this time the Herrera family had moved to New York where Herrera's husband was special projects editor at *Vanity Fair* magazine. Herrera told a reporter for *Newsweek* that once she opened her House of Herrera design firm, she "changed from being a mother with nothing to do but arrange flowers and parties to being a professional who works twelve hours a day at the office."

Her first collection stunned the fashion world. Many expected Herrera to be a frivolous socialite with nothing of real substance to contribute to the fashion business. She proved them wrong when her glamorous dresses and gowns—of many different fabrics, layers, and lengths—appealed to other socialites like herself.

Dresses the Rich and Famous

Within two years, Herrera received worldwide acclaim. Many well-known political figures and celebrities began to wear her creations. Among her customers were former U.S. first ladies Jacqueline Onassis and Nancy Reagan, Princess Elizabeth of Yugoslavia, Spain's Duchess of Feria, and American actress Kathleen Turner. Traveling in the same international social circles as these famous people, Herrera understands their lifestyles and designs clothes to fit their needs and desires.

The fine quality and unique designs of Herrera's clothes make them much in demand in spite of their exceptional prices. In 1982, a luncheon suit by Herrera cost anywhere between $1,500 and $3,800. Silk pajamas made especially for lounging at the pool were tagged at $1,200. Her exquisite gowns ranged from $2,100 to $4,000. Fortunately for the rest of society, other designers have copied her styles and made their imitations available at lesser prices.

In 1987 Herrera was bestowed the MODA award as the Top Hispanic Designer by Hispanic Designers, Inc. Previous winners include the famous designers Aldolfo and Oscar de La Renta. In the late 1980s Herrera branched out to design a sportswear line for younger women, a leather and fur collection, and a less expensive line of clothing that she named "CH." She also introduced her own perfumes, "Carolina Herrera," and "Flore." The jasmine and tuberose fragrance of "Carolina Herrera" reminds Herrera of her happy childhood—a jasmine vine grew in the family garden and scented her bedroom.

Despite her wealth and worldliness, Herrera leads a simple life. She walks to her New York office each day, accompanied by her dog, Alfonso. She works an eight-hour day, and often attends a charity event in the evening. Even though she has earned her place as a distinguished fashion designer, Herrera continues to work hard. "I am never

Carolina Herrera

satisfied," she told an interviewer for *Hispanic*. "I'm a perfectionist. When I see the show is ready and the collection is out and they're quite nice, I still say, 'I could do much better.'"

For Further Information

Americas, September/October 1990, pp. 30-35.
Hispanic, March 1989, pp. 28-32; October 1989, pp. 36-37.
Newsweek, June 30, 1986, pp. 56-57.
Vogue, January 1991, p. 132.

Oscar Hijuelos

Writer
Born August 24, 1951, New York, New York

"What I want to do is entertain and give readers something that can help them live more happily, just like characters in a song of love."

In 1990 Oscar Hijuelos became the first Hispanic writer to publish a book that received the Pulitzer Prize for fiction, America's highest literary award. His novel *The Mambo Kings Play Songs of Love,* which won the award, explores the lives of two Cuban brothers who seek fame as musicians in the United States during the 1950s. Hijuelos's book portrays the impact of Hispanic influences on American popular culture in a way that American fiction has neglected in the past.

Hijuelos was born in New York City in 1951. His parents, Pascual and Magdalena Torrens Hijuelos, had emigrated from Cuba to the United States in 1943. The family owned some farmland and two factories in their homeland, but Hijuelos's father lost what money they had after they went to America. "He was very generous, trusting to a fault," Hijuelos related to Dinitia Smith in *New York,* adding, "Occasionally, he liked to drink too much."

Although they lived in a culturally rich neighborhood that included people of Jewish, Italian, Irish, and African American descent, the Hijuelos family spoke only Spanish at home. When he was three years old, Hijuelos visited Cuba with his family. He contracted nephritis—a serious infection of the kidneys—during the trip, and after returning to the United States he was sent to a hospital for terminally ill children in Connecticut. Hijuelos spent two years there before finally recovering. During this time, he learned to speak English.

After high school, Hijuelos attended Bronx Community College. He later transferred to the City College of the City University of New York, where he earned his bachelor's degree in English in 1975. The following year he received his master's degree in creative writing. While enrolled in City College's distinguished graduate writing program, he studied creative writing with noted author Donald Barthelme, who is best known for his short stories.

Follows His Dream

Hijuelos then obtained a job with Transportation Display Inc., an advertising firm in New York that creates ads for subways and buses. At night, he pursued his dream of being a writer, penning short stories and sending them to magazines for publication. His fiction quickly gained notice, and he was awarded grants, fellowships, and scholarships from such prestigious writing associations as the Breadloaf Writers Conference.

By 1983 Hijuelos had written enough material to publish his first novel, *Our House in the Last World.* The book follows the lives of the Santinios, a Cuban family, as they immigrate to America in the 1940s. As they struggle to adapt to life in the United States, the Santinios also try to hold on to their cultural past and maintain their identities as Cubans in America.

Critical reaction to *Our House in the Last World* was enthusiastic. Many reviewers saw Hijuelos's writing style as elegant and moving and praised the book for its vivid and compassionate depiction of the immigrant experience—especially of the sense of alienation so often felt by people who leave their homeland to settle in a foreign country. Both the National Endowment for the Arts and the American Academy and Institute of Arts and Letters awarded the author fellowships for his book. The money from these awards allowed him to quit his day job and devote his time completely to writing.

Second Novel Focuses on Two Brothers

Hijuelos finished work on his second novel, *The Mambo Kings Play Songs of Love,* in 1989. The novel tells the story of Cesar and Nestor Castillo, two musician brothers who leave Cuba in 1949 and seek their fortune on New York's nightclub circuit. Latin dance music was catching on in the United States by the early 1950s, and Hijuelos captures the mood of the era in his narrative.

The Castillo brothers form an orchestra to play in nightclubs where people dance the mambo, a rhythmic dance set to horns and drums. Their only big hit is "Beautiful María of My Soul," a romantic song Nestor has rewritten 22 times about his love for a woman he left behind in Cuba. The highlight of the brothers' career occurs when they are invited by bandleader Desi Arnaz (see **Desi Arnaz**) to perform their song on the hit television show *I Love Lucy.*

But soon after this, the Latin dance craze begins to fade and the brothers' lives spiral

Oscar Hijuelos

downward. Even though he is married to another woman, Nestor cannot forget his lost love. With each passing year, he becomes more withdrawn and eventually dies of heartbreak. Cesar, a heavy drinker and womanizer, ends his days as a superintendent of a run-down hotel. Through a drunken haze, he dreams of his past glory days.

Mambo Kings Wins Top Award

Farrar, Straus & Giroux, the publisher of *The Mambo Kings Play Songs of Love,* made the book its lead fall title in 1989. It was the first time a major publishing house had ever invested heavily in a Hispanic writer. The book became a best-seller and was nominated for both the National Book Award and the National Book Critics Award, two of America's top literary awards. In 1990 *The*

Mambo Kings was awarded the Pulitzer Prize. A film version of the novel, starring Armand Assante and Antonio Banderas and featuring the music of Tito Puente (see **Tito Puente**), was released in 1992.

Despite the somber ending of *The Mambo Kings* and the main characters' seemingly tragic preoccupation with the past, Hijuelos believes his role as a novelist is to enlighten and uplift his readers. "People live this dream and then they hit real life again.... What I want to do is entertain and give readers something that can help them live more happily," he told an interviewer in *Publishers Weekly*, "just like characters in a song of love."

Hijuelos's third novel, *The Fourteen Sisters of Emilio Montez O'Brien,* was published in 1993. Set in the United States at the beginning of the twentieth century, the story centers on the lives of 14 sisters, their Cuban mother, and their Irish father. Through the book, Hijuelos tries to present "a pure appreciation of the *female* principle of life, the nurturing things," he explained to Smith in *New York.* "The things that are the most beautiful in the world are mostly female."

For Further Information

Detroit News, September 3, 1989.
Hispanic Writers, Gale, 1991, pp. 255-256.
Newsweek, August 21, 1989.
New York, March 1, 1993, pp. 46-51.
New York Times, September 11, 1989.
New York Times Book Review, August 27, 1989, pp. 1, 30.
Publishers Weekly, July 21, 1989.
Washington Post, August 20, 1989.

Dolores Huerta

Labor leader, social activist
Born April 10, 1930, Dawson, New Mexico

"I think we brought to the world, the United States anyway, the whole idea of boycotting as a nonviolent tactic. I think we showed the world that nonviolence can work to make social change."

Dolores Huerta is the most prominent Chicana (Mexican American woman) labor leader in the United States. She is cofounder and first vice president of the United Farm Workers union. For more than thirty years she has dedicated her life to the struggle for justice and dignity for migrant farm workers. Honored with countless community service, labor, Hispanic, and women's awards, Huerta is a role model for Mexican American women.

Dolores Fernández Huerta was born in 1930 in the small mining town of Dawson in northern New Mexico. She was the second child and only daughter of Juan Fernández and Alicia Cháves Fernández. Her mother's parents had been born in New Mexico, while her father's parents had immigrated to America from Mexico. When Huerta was a toddler her parents divorced, and she moved to California with her mother and two brothers.

As a single parent during the Great Depression (a severe economic slowdown in America during the 1930s), Alicia Cháves Fernández had a difficult time supporting her young family. While she worked at a cannery at night and as a waitress during the day, her father helped watch the children. The young Huerta enjoyed a close relationship with her grandfather. "My grandfather used to call me seven tongues," she related to Margaret Rose in *Notable Hispanic American Women,* "because I always talked so much." As Huerta grew older, her mother encouraged her to get involved in youth activities. She took violin, piano, and dance lessons. She also sang in the church choir and was an active Girl Scout.

During the 1940s her family's financial situation improved. Huerta's mother, who had remarried, now owned a restaurant and hotel. Huerta and her brothers helped run these establishments. She believes she learned to appreciate all different types of people while growing up and working in an ethnically diverse neighborhood. Her community included Japanese, Chinese, Jewish, Filipino, and Mexican families.

Dolores Huerta

Inspired by Father's Accomplishments

Although Huerta was separated from her father, she did not lose contact with him. His work activities inspired her. To supplement his wages as a coal miner, he joined the migrant labor force, traveling to Colorado, Nebraska, and Wyoming. He was unhappy with working conditions and became active in labor unions. He eventually returned to school to earn a college degree. In 1938 he won election to the New Mexico state legislature where he worked for better labor laws. Huerta was proud of her father's education, his union activism, and his political achievements.

Huerta attended schools in her hometown of Stockton, California. Then, unlike most Hispanic women of her generation, she went on to college. She earned a teaching certificate, but was frustrated with the limitations of the job. She realized she wanted to do more than just teach children. She wanted to help those who came to school barefoot and hungry.

Huerta soon found her niche in community work and social activism. In the mid-1950s, she began to work for the Community Service Organization (CSO), a Mexican-American self-help association founded in Los Angeles. She registered people to vote, organized citizenship classes for immigrants, and pressed local governments for improvements in barrios (Spanish-speaking neighborhoods). As a result of her skills, the CSO sent her to the California capital of Sacramento to work as a lobbyist (a person who persuades legislators to vote for certain laws). Then, during the late 1950s, Huerta became concerned about the living and working conditions of farm workers.

Since before World War II, life for migrant farm workers had been incredibly harsh. They worked in the hot sun for hours, picking crops such as grapes, tomatoes, and cotton. During the often cool nights, they slept in run-down shacks or in their cars if they could not afford a room. Farm owners paid the workers poor wages. Sometimes workers were paid fifty cents for every basket they picked. Other times they were paid only twenty cents. Some owners paid even less, subtracting from a worker's pay for any water he or she drank in the fields during the hot day. Many of the workers were Mexicans or Mexican Americans who knew little English. Farm owners often took advantage of this, swindling the workers out of the money they had rightfully earned for their day's hard labor.

Chávez and the UFW

Huerta joined the Agricultural Workers Association, a community interest group in northern California. Through her work with the AWA, she met César Chávez (see **César Chávez**), the director of the CSO in California and Arizona. Chávez shared her deep interest in farm workers. Unhappy with the CSO's unwillingness to form a union for farm workers, Chávez and Huerta eventually branched off to found the National Farm Workers Association in Delano, California, in 1962. After 1972 this influential union would be known simply as the United Farm Workers (UFW).

As second-in-command to Chávez, Huerta helped shape and guide the union. In 1965, when Delano grape workers went on strike, she devised the strategy for the strike and led the workers on the picket lines. Afterward, she became the union's first contract negotiator. In the late 1960s, she directed the grape boycott on the east coast, the primary distribution point for grapes. Her work there helped bring about a successful grape boycott across the nation.

Huerta's style was forceful and uncompromising. However, she succeeded in bringing together feminists, community workers, religious groups, Hispanic associations, student protestors, and peace groups. All were united to fight for the rights of migrant farm workers. Victory finally came in 1975 when California Governor Jerry Brown signed the Agricultural Labor Relations Act. This was the first bill of rights for farm workers ever enacted in America. It legally allowed them to form a union that would negotiate with farm owners for better wages and working conditions.

UFW Activities Prove Dangerous

Over the years, Huerta has committed her energies to the UFW as a leader, speaker, fund raiser, negotiator, picket captain, and advisor to government leaders. In the 1980s she helped found KUFW—Radio Campesina, the union's radio station in California. She continued testifying before state and federal committees on a range of issues, including the use of pesticides on crops and other health matters facing migrant workers.

Many of Huerta's activities on behalf of the UFW have placed her in personal danger.

She has been arrested more than 20 times. In 1988, during a peaceful demonstration in San Francisco against the policies of presidential candidate George Bush, Huerta was severely injured by baton-swinging police officers. She suffered two broken ribs and a ruptured spleen. In order to save her life, she had to undergo emergency surgery. This incident outraged the public and caused the San Francisco police department to change its rules regarding crowd control and discipline.

After recovering from her life-threatening injuries, Huerta resumed her work on behalf of farm workers in the 1990s. She firmly believes the accomplishments of the UFW will continue to benefit the Hispanic community. "I think we brought to the world, the United States anyway, the whole idea of boycotting as a nonviolent tactic," she told Rose. "I think we showed the world that nonviolence can work to make social change."

For Further Information

De Ruiz, Dana Catharine, and Richard Larios, *La Causa: The Migrant Farmworkers' Story*, Raintree Steck-Vaughn, 1992.

Dunne, John Gregory, *Delano: The Story of the California Grape Strike*, Farrar, 1976.

Notable Hispanic American Women, Gale Research, 1993.

National Catholic Reporter, September 30, 1988, p. 12.

Julio Iglesias

Singer, songwriter
Born September 23, 1943, Madrid, Spain

"The biggest problem in my job is that you get afraid to lose it. One day you are a winner, but the next, no matter how big of a star you are, you can be a loser."

Spanish singer Julio Iglesias has sold more albums than any other singer in the world—more than 175 million as of 1992. His fame first began when his Spanish songs and romantic style won audiences in his homeland and in Latin American countries. When Iglesias started singing in Portuguese, Italian, French, German, Japanese, and English, his fan club quickly spread around the world.

Julio José Iglesias de la Cueva was born in 1943 in Madrid, Spain, to Julio Iglesias, Sr., a wealthy gynecologist, and his wife, Rosario. He had a comfortable childhood. While growing up, he attended Catholic schools, where his grades were mediocre and he couldn't sing well enough to join the school choir. One thing he did excel at, however, was soccer. After he graduated from high school, he briefly studied law at the University of Madrid, but gave it up to become goalie for Real Madrid, Spain's premier professional soccer team.

Accident Ends Soccer Career

Iglesias's athletic career was cut short in 1963 when he was almost killed in an automobile accident. After his car had been

Julio Iglesias

Vida Sigue Igual" ("Life Goes on Just the Same"). He performed it at the 1968 Festival de la Canción, a national singing competition in Spain, and won first prize. He then recorded the song and it became a hit on Spanish radio. To please his parents, Iglesias completed law school, but then concentrated his energies on music. By 1971 he had signed a recording contract with Alhambra Records, and his voice hit the airwaves throughout Europe, Japan, and Latin America.

That same year, Iglesias married Isabel Preysler, who came from a wealthy Phillipine family. The couple eventually had three children: Chabeli, Julio José, and Enrique. Although Iglesias and Preysler divorced in 1979, Iglesias has remained close to his children. His career, however, is his main passion. "He was always into his work," Chabeli explained to Cynthia Sanz in *People*. "When he had the time, he was with us, but family was never his strong point."

Perfectionist in the Studio

Iglesias, who spends up to nine months a year in the recording studio, earned a reputation as a workaholic and a perfectionist. It was not uncommon for him to sing a particular song over and over in the studio until he was satisfied. His dedication to his craft paid off: By 1973 he had sold ten million albums. In 1980 his album *Hey* was the number one album in 80 countries.

In 1983 Iglesias had six albums on the pop charts, a feat managed previously only by Elvis Presley and the Beatles. That year, he earned a spot in the *Guinness Book of World Records* for having sold 100 million records in six languages (Iglesias is fluent in

forced off the road by a runaway truck, it rolled over several times. Iglesias's spine was injured in the accident. For a week, he was in a coma. For the next year, he was paralyzed from the chest down. Iglesias knew his sports career was over, but he was determined not to spend his life in a wheelchair. He underwent physical therapy for the next three years. To help keep his mind off his disabilities during his long recovery, his soccer teammates gave him a guitar. After learning a few chords, he began to play along with songs on the radio. Soon he was composing songs of his own.

Iglesias regained the use of his legs, but was left with a slight, permanent limp. Since playing soccer was out, he focused on singing as a career. On a trip to England to improve his English, he composed the song "La

Spanish, French, Italian, Portuguese, and English).

Despite having switched to the larger CBS International record company in 1980, Iglesias still found it difficult to reach an English-speaking audience. Finally, British tourists in Spain in the early 1980s took note of his popularity and brought his records home to British disc jockeys. Iglesias soon became the first Hispanic singer to have a number one song in England—the Spanish-language version of Cole Porter's "Begin the Beguine." CBS began to release his albums in English and book him on talk shows in the United States.

Duets Bring Him a U.S. Audience

Iglesias's first album in English was the 1984 release *1100 Bel Air Place*. The record, which featured duets with American stars Diana Ross, the Beach Boys, and the Pointer Sisters, sold four million copies in the United States. He then went on to earn a country-western audience when his duet with Willie Nelson, "To All the Girls I've Loved Before," became a hit.

Even though Iglesias has remained more popular outside of the United States, he has come to embrace the country. "This is an incredible country," he told Achy Obejas in *Hispanic*. "It's very special to me. But perhaps it's something else too. People who don't have a home can make a home anywhere." Iglesias mirrors this feeling of goodwill by supporting many charities around the world. Since the beginning of his career, he has donated more than $20 million to health and social service organizations. In the United States, he supports the American

Paralysis Association, the Red Cross, and Casita Maria, a New York-based organization for Hispanic unwed mothers.

Iglesias performs about 200 stage shows per year, jetting between countries in his private plane. He owns a ranch in Argentina and a mansion in Miami. Despite his many fans and successes, however, Iglesias knows that the fame he has achieved over the years can one day suddenly fade away. Memories of his accident remind him of that. "The biggest problem in my job is that you get afraid to lose it," he explained to Dougherty. "One day you are a winner, but the next, no matter how big of a star you are, you can be a loser."

For Further Information

Hispanic, August 1988, pp. 26-30; May 1991, pp. 20-26.
People, August 29, 1988, pp. 50-54; November 23, 1993, pp. 63-64; May 23, 1994, p. 23.
TV Guide, November 24, 1990, pp. 20-22.

Raul Julia

Actor
Born March 9, 1940, San Juan, Puerto Rico
Died October 24, 1994, Manhasset, New York

"I like to explore. I always have the sense that there must be something more ... that there are possibilities we don't even know about."

Raul Julia was an actor well known for his broad range of talents. From his work in classic stage productions such as William Shakespeare's tragedy *Othello* to zany film comedies like *The Addams Family,* Julia earned praise from critics—and from audiences of all ages. Whatever role he took on, he felt compelled to probe his character's background, feelings, and beliefs; such attention to detail became his trademark in the industry. What was most important for Julia, though, was constantly testing his own acting abilities. "I love diversity in acting," he explained to Phoebe Hoban in *New York* magazine, adding that he was most interested in "trying to do things I'm not sure I can do."

Raul Rafael Carlos Julia y Arcelay was born in San Juan, Puerto Rico, in 1940, the oldest of four children of Raul and Olga Julia. Before Julia was born, his father studied electrical engineering in the United States. After returning to San Juan, the elder Julia opened a gas station, then a chicken and pizza restaurant. Both of his parents wanted their young son to grow up to become a lawyer, but he had a different idea early in life.

Julia had his first role on the stage at the age of five, playing the devil in a school play. From that moment on he was hooked. While attending parochial schools (private schools maintained by a religious body) in San Juan, he performed in every school play that was staged. After he graduated from high school, he enrolled in the University of Puerto Rico, eventually earning a bachelor of arts degree. He then moved to New York City in the mid-1960s to study acting. For a while, he had to live on money his parents sent to him. After he won his first role in the Spanish play *Life Is a Dream,* he was able to support himself, but times remained tough.

Brings Shakespeare to Hispanic Neighborhoods

To save money, Julia shared a tiny apartment with another actor. Because he could not get work in the theater, he often performed in small plays on the street. More than once he was hit with eggs and bottles thrown by rude, unappreciative audiences. In 1967 he landed a role in a Spanish mobile-theater production of Shakespeare's *Macbeth.* He and the rest of the cast traveled through New York neighborhoods in a truck that turned into a stage. Julia was happy not only to have work but to bring theater to people who didn't have the time or the money to see plays in New York's theater district.

This role led to others, but Julia still had a hard time earning money. For a while he tried to sell magazines and pens, but his heart wasn't in it. He then worked as a house (theater) manager for the New York Shakespeare Festival. He was happy to do anything connected with theater. Occasionally he was even allowed to play a small role in the Festival's productions.

Julia's big break came in 1971 when he received the role of Proteus in a production of Shakespeare's *Two Gentlemen of Verona.* Originally staged in New York City's Central Park, the production became a hit after it moved to Broadway. Julia's performance caught the attention of theater critics, and he was nominated for a Tony Award (the equivalent of the film world's Academy Award). Over the next decade, he played larger, more demanding roles in such theatrical productions as Shakespeare's *Hamlet* and Kurt Weill's *Threepenny Opera.* His work brought three more Tony Award nominations.

Raul Julia

Researches His Roles Thoroughly

During this time Julia began branching out into television and motion pictures. For a while, his work in movies was limited to small roles that did not attract much attention. In 1985, however, he achieved stardom for his portrayal of a South American political prisoner in *Kiss of the Spider Woman,* a film that also starred William Hurt. To ready himself for the role, Julia talked to Brazilians who had actually been imprisoned or tortured because of their political beliefs. "I needed to know what the feelings and emotions were of a person who had gone through that," he noted in the *New York* interview with Hoban. "You feel humiliated. You feel anger. And you cannot express it."

Similarly, Julia spent countless hours preparing for other roles. When he portrayed a lawyer in the whodunit *Presumed Innocent,* he spent days in court with a criminal attorney to become familiar with the legal system and the courtroom environment. And for his role as Archbishop Oscar Romero of El Salvador in the film *Romero,* he listened to the priest's actual taped sermons and diaries.

Julia's in-depth research often changed his outlook on his own life—affecting him even after the cameras had stopped rolling. He was, for example, raised a Catholic but had drifted away from his religion as he grew older. His research for *Romero* required him to delve back into Catholicism and brought about a renewal of his faith. After filming was completed, Julia became a practicing Catholic once again.

In the 1990s Julia became something of a household name as the charmingly eccentric Gomez Addams in two films based on the popular comic strips of Charles Addams. In September of 1994 he portrayed Brazilian labor unionist Chico Mendes in the cable television film *The Burning Season.* Julia's last film was the Universal release *Street Fighter.*

Julia was married to Merel Poloway, and had two sons, Raul Sigmund and Benjamin Rafael. When he was not acting, Julia worked for Project Hunger, a group devoted to finding ways to end world hunger by the year 2000. With each new role on the stage, on television, and in films, he continued to receive acclaim. His only requirement for himself as an actor was that he never stand still. "I like to explore," he told Hoban. "I always have the sense that there must be something more … that there are possibilities we don't even know about."

The world was shocked when it was revealed that Julia, only 54, had fallen into a coma after sustaining a stroke on October 16, 1994. He died twelve days later. Though many knew him primarily through his role as Gomez Addams, he is remembered by his peers as a gifted actor who never stopped striving for excellence in the variety of roles he tackled.

For Further Information

America, February 25, 1989, p. 164.
New York, November 25, 1991, pp. 52-56.
New York Times, October 24, 1994, B15.
Stefoff, Rebecca, *Raul Julia: Puerto Rican Actor,* Chelsea House, 1994.

FIELD OF ENDEAVOR INDEX

MEDICINE

Lifshitz, Aliza **2**
Novello, Antonia **2**

MUSIC

Arnaz, Desi **1**
Baez, Joan **1**
Blades, Rubén **1**
Casals, Pablo **1**
Domingo, Placido **1**
E., Sheila **1**
Estefan, Gloria **1**
Feliciano, José **1**
Garcia, Jerry **1**
Iglesias, Julio **1**
Los Lobos **2**
Mata, Eduardo **2**
Moreno, Rita **2**
Puente, Tito **2**
Ronstadt, Linda **2**
Santana, Carlos **2**
Valens, Ritchie **2**

RELIGION

Las Casas, Bartolomé de **2**
Serra, Junípero **2**

SCIENCE AND TECHNOLOGY

Ochoa, Ellen **2**

SOCIAL ACTIVISM

Baez, Joan **1**
Capetillo, Luisa **1**
Castillo, Sylvia L. **1**
Chávez, César **1**
Gonzalez, Rodolfo "Corky" **1**
Hernández, Antonia **1**
Huerta, Dolores **1**
Martí, José **2**
Rodríguez, Gloria **2**
Tijerina, Reies López **2**
Zapata, Emiliano **2**

SPORTS

Bonilla, Bobby **1**
Canseco, José **1**
Casals, Rosemary **1**
Clemente, Roberto **1**
Fernández, Mary Joe **1**
Gonzalez, Juan **1**
Gonzalez, Rodolfo "Corky" **1**
Hernandez, Guillermo
   (Willie) **1**
Lopez, Nancy **2**
Lucero-Schayes, Wendy **2**
McLish, Rachel **2**
Ortiz-Del Valle, Sandra **2**
Plunkett, James **2**
Rodríguez, Juan "Chi Chi" **2**
Treviño, Lee **2**

TELEVISION

Arnaz, Desi **1**
Carter, Lynda Cordoba **1**
Manzano, Sonia **2**
Moreno, Rita **2**
Olmos, Edward James **2**
Peña, Elizabeth **2**
Rivera, Geraldo **2**
Rodríguez, Paul **2**
Saralegui, Cristina **2**
Welch, Raquel **2**

THEATER

Ronstadt, Linda **2**
Valdez, Luis **2**